Memoirs of an Old White History Teacher

~

Plus 20 True-False Questions and Some American History in One Easy Read

~

By VIRGINIA BERNHARD

AN INDEPENDENT PUBLICATION

OTHER BOOKS BY VIRGINIA BERNHARD

A College History of the United States

Firsthand America: A History of the United States

The Smell of War: Three Americans in the Trenches of World War I

Jamestown: The Novel

The Hoggs of Texas: Letters and Memoirs of an Extraordinary Family

A Tale of Two Colonies: What Really Happened in Early Virginia and Bermuda?

Ima Hogg: The Governor's Daughter

Slaves and Slaveholders in Bermuda, 1616-1782

A Durable Fire

Memoirs of an Old
White History Teacher

$\mathbf{Y}$ears before Black Lives Matter, before George Floyd, before Covid turned everything upside down, before January 6, 2021, and before the 2022 war in Ukraine, I taught U.S. history to college students. Every year for thirty-five years I taught what many history professors regard as a bore and a chore: the U.S. Survey: "U.S. History to 1877" and "U.S. History Since 1877."

That was long before cancel culture, critical race theory, being woke, book banning, vote suppressing, and the Big Steal. These are fighting words to many. But before you throw this book against the wall, give it a chance. You may learn stuff that will surprise you.

These days, being retired from teaching since 2006, I have plenty of time to read, and I am often disturbed, saddened, and even alarmed by the news. Sometimes I save clippings—Yes, I still read real paper newspapers.

"America began with a crime—stealing the land from Native Americans."

That was long before the Big Steal of 2020.
But wait. There's more to this quote:

It continued with an atrocity, slavery. The American story is the conflict between oppressors who seek to preserve white supremacy and people who seek to move beyond it. The essential American struggle is to confront the national sin, have a racial reckoning and then move beyond it."

—David Brooks,
The New York Times, June 6, 2019.

Some years before this, in fact, eleven years before, I saved a quote from an aspiring presidential candidate. In a historic speech on March 18, 2008, he opened the dark closet of "our tragic history" and pulled out the skeletons of slavery and racism. When Barack Obama won that presidential election with "Yes, We Can," many people felt as if the biggest stain on our history had been wiped away. No, Not Yet.

In thirty-five years of teaching American history classes, I watched my students confront the skeletons—racism and slavery—in our nation's closet. Year after year I did my best to help my classes to come to terms with America's past.

I felt the anguish of a student who crouched low at his desk and hid his face in his hands when we discussed the use of the N-word.

I laughed with a class crowded elbow to elbow into a stifling-hot exam room when a student said, "Hey, man, this is like a slave ship!"

I shuddered when a student whose part-time job was cooking fast-food hamburgers wrote that she spit into the patties she made for white people.

I was moved as a student wept when she learned that nightriders fired shots into Fannie Lou Hamer's share-cropper house in Mississippi.

I tried to comfort a student who came to my office and said, "I just want to find out who I am!"

All of these students were African Americans, college freshmen.

They were few in number, adrift in a sea of white students at the University of St. Thomas in Houston. Some of them sailed confidently, but others did not. In the class that discussed the N word, the student who hid his face always sat in the back and never entered into any discussions. He lay low and never raised his hand. I was afraid he would melt into the floor if I dared to call on him. I never could catch him to chat after class, either. He fled at the sound of the bell. I felt that a note from me to him would only make him more uncomfortable. I wonder what became of him.

What was I to do? Something was wrong here, and it went deeper than just a situation with one student in one American history class. The bones of the skeleton were sticking out. That student was one of two Black faces in that class of 25. The other Black face belonged to a cheerful young woman with granny glasses and a head full of cornrows. Her hand was always up, and she was far from shy. She agreed that the N-word had its place, mainly among Blacks themselves, but that books like *Huckleberry Finn* were historical and ought not to be banned for using it. She will be OK, I thought. I wonder what became of her.

My older African American students also astonished me. I was awestruck, along with the rest of my History of the Family in America class, when a student told us she'd found in the U.S. census records the identity of the mysterious "Aunt Tennie" her family had always spoken of in hushed tones. Now, with wide eyes and solemn face, this student announced that

"Aunt Tennie was a slave."

Those words hung in the air, and those of us who heard it sat stunned and silent. This was not a word in a history book. This was a word connected to a real person. My students, and as a matter of fact, I, had never come this close to slavery. We learned that Aunt Tennie was born a slave on a Louisiana plantation just before the Civil War. As a free woman afterwards, she married and had a family. Her descendants knew that, but they never said the word "slave" out loud. More than a hundred years later, they didn't want anybody to know. They were still ashamed.

Another African American student in that same family history class brought some tattered black-and-white photos of her grandfather's sharecropper family picking cotton in Mississippi. Amid rows and rows of cotton plants blooming with fluffy white bolls, dark-skinned men and women and children stooped under the weight of heavy cotton sacks.

"Cotton bolls are sharp. When you pick them they cut into your hands," this student said. "My grandpa told me that." None of us hearing her had ever picked cotton. Our views of cotton-picking came from *Gone With the Wind*, with happy slaves singing in three-part harmony.

I was appalled to learn that many other African American students simply did not know their own history. In a seminar on the

1960s and the civil rights movement (this was a class in the 1980s), an excited young African American woman confessed that she had never heard of Martin Luther King, Jr. "Neither has my boyfriend," she said, "I can't wait to tell him." Something is wrong here, I said to myself.

My students were not the only ones trying to make sense of the past. At a Southern women's history conference in the 1980s, young African American women scholars shouted angrily at white women scholars who presented papers on Black women's history. Several conference sessions almost came to blows.

"How dare you write about us!"

"You cannot possibly know what we know!"

"You have no right to our history!"

Feelings simmered. Knots of angry people glared at each other in hallways. But by the end of that three-day conference 40 years ago, all of us, a mix of some 300 white and black women and men, sat on the grass on a warm summer evening, holding hands and swaying as we sang, "We Shall Overcome."

That was then. This is now, and we still have not overcome.

The skeletons keep falling out of the closet. Like Fibber McGee in in the 1940s radio program that only old people remember, we open the closet door and everything in it tumbles out. Every one of us has our own closet of memories that shape us, that steer us in certain directions. I want to explore mine, to see how I got here. That is why I'm writing this memoir.

> *History doesn't happen to cultures.*
> *It doesn't happen to races.*
> *It happens to people.*
> --George C. Wolfe, American playwright

I put this quotation in the opening pages of my 1999 book about the history of slavery in Bermuda. I think about it often these days.

I also think about the time I was invited to lecture about my slavery book in Bermuda. There was an audience of about 200 that evening, most of them Blacks. Bermuda, after all, is a country with a population two-thirds Black. They, like the young Black scholars at the women's history conference, were angry that a white woman, and a non-Bermudian at that, had dared to write about their history. In the question-and-answer period after my lecture, many in the audience were hostile. I was OK with that. I wished we could all go somewhere and have a drink and talk things over. Finally the director of the Bermuda National Museum (a white guy) stood up, turned to face the audience, and said, "If you don't like her book, write your own!"

My first memory of a Black face was my grandmother's cook Carrie, a jolly, no-nonsense woman built like a refrigerator. She used to shoo two five-year-olds, my cousin and me, out of her kitchen by giving us slabs of white bread slathered with Miracle Whip. "Out of here, you! I'm busy!" she would say, and then go back to rolling out biscuits. We adored her.

When I started first grade in Austin, Texas, in the 1940s I saw only white faces. Same for when we moved to Fort Stockton, Texas. In that little West Texas town back then, I don't think there were any Blacks. The only non-white faces belonged to Mexican Americans. There were a lot of them. Their school was a brick building on the other side of the football field from our school. Nobody thought that was peculiar. Fort Stockton was a town of adobe as well as brick and wood buildings. It was a bilingual town. In stores and restaurants, English and Spanish flowed easily back and forth. In schools, Mexican kids learned English, and we Anglos learned Spanish. That was long before Bilingual Education. I still remember the words to "Oh Where, Oh Where Has My Little Dog Gone?" en español. I learned them in the second grade. (Note: grade school children can pick up other languages quite easily.)

When I was eight, my family moved to Gilmer, a little East Texas town where there were lots of Black faces, and we had a Black maid named Ura. The first day she came to work, my mother set the table for three and said, "Ura, it's lunch time."

Ura said, "Oh, no ma'am. I cain't sit down with white folks."

My mother, born and bred in East Texas, said, "Oh yes you can. Sit!" Ura sat. She became my best friend. Taught me to play checkers (She let me win once in a while.). Gave me a kitten from a litter born at her house, which I often visited. Ura lived across the railroad tracks from our part of town, but in those days whites and Blacks crossed back and forth with no thought of danger.

I think my mother got her views about race from her father. Some family stories about him: A Black woman named Ethel, a single mom with two little boys, worked as a maid and lived in a little house behind my grandparents' house in Tenaha, Texas. One day Ethel's boys came to see my grandfather and told him that "a white man been botherin' our mama at night."

"I'll take care of it," said my grandfather. His name was Ferrin Stanley, and he was a big man, six feet three inches and 250 pounds. What he did, he never said, and nobody knows, but Ethel was not bothered any more.

When several Black men in Tenaha told "Mr. Ferrin," as everybody called him, that the feed store owner was putting rocks in their feed sacks and charging full weight, he said, "Bring me one of your sacks." He went to the owner's office and dumped the sack full of rocks and feed on the owner's desk. As the rocks rattled down, my grandfather said, "Do this again, and I'll dump a bag like this on you at First Baptist Church during a service." There were no more rocks in feed sacks.

Ferrin Stanley once ran for sheriff in that East Texas county, but he didn't win. Later in his life he was the house detective at the Driskill Hotel in Austin, Texas. He never told stories about what he did there, but I wish he had. He did tell about a time in Tenaha in the 1920s when the Ku Klux Klan was having a revival in Texas. A bunch of Tenaha men decided to organize a chapter. They got their white robes and hoods, and talked about which black people's yards they would burn a cross in—but they couldn't agree on which ones.

"Oh, no, not X! He's a good old fella."

"We can't do Y! They have six young 'uns."

"Not Z! His wife works for us."

At long last, they quietly put away their robes and disbanded their group.

My grandfather was never among them. More about him later.

My other early memories about race and culture are about Native Americans, but they belong to another part of this book. Meanwhile, some thoughts about how most of us learned American history.

Most people have grown up with American history as a set of stories about brave white settlers who came to a New World, conquered a wilderness, and built a nation dedicated to liberty and justice for all. ("All" here means whites. Blacks and Native Americans and others need not apply.)

The Native Americans (who had been living here a long, long time) did not call the newcomers "whites." At first they were simply "foreigners." How do I know? My friend Alden Vaughan, a distinguished historian and author of a shelf full of colonial history books, told me. I had asked him to look over a draft of my historical novel about early Virginia. I mailed him a hard copy (this was before email did away with boxy manuscripts sent by snail mail) in New York. He read it and phoned me (this was before texting and facetime). "Get rid of the white men," he said. Thank goodness for search-and-replace. I could get rid of "white men" and "whites" in my novel, but the real whites in American history are nearly all of the story.

Until the 1960s, that story was largely written by white males.

As scholarship has grown more and more diverse, (Diverse nowadays is a code word for non-white) a different American history is showing up. Like a mole in landscaped lawn, it pokes its snout up and disturbs the smooth surface. It digs up some unpleasant dirt. For example, think of the recent flap over a 2021 book called *Forget the Alamo: The Rise and Fall of an American Myth* by Bryan Burrough, Chris Tomlinson, and Jason Stanford. All they did was to poke some holes in the Noble-White-Guys-versus-Nasty-Mexicans story.

The Alamo story clearly touched a nerve, but not nearly as painful a nerve as the one about this nation's earlier history. Now something called "critical race theory" has set many people's teeth on edge. State boards of education and local school boards and teachers and parents are yelling at each other in meetings. Is slavery to blame for all of American history? Will learning about racism make white students feel bad? How should we teach the history of the United States? And more important, who's going to decide? State officials? School boards? Teachers? Parents? This is a question that's not going away any time soon.

11

Let's look at the history: School integration began after the 1954 landmark Supreme Court decision in Brown v. Board of Education said that "separate but equal" schools were not equal at all. Many parents in those days were upset. Here's a personal memory: In the 1960s and 70s lots of parents snatched their kids out of public schools and put them in private (all-white) schools. That was known as "white flight." Our three children attended public schools from first grade to high school in Houston. Yes, they met a number of African American kids, and no, the world did not end. They made friends. I don't recall ever having a family discussion about race in so many words. We took it easy. When our son Paul ran for class president in high school, his opponent was an African American guy. The two of them cracked jokes about it: "Who you vote for as Class President depends on whether you want a short white guy or a tall Black guy." P.S. They both ran for class president two years in a row. One year the Black guy won, and the next year, the white guy won.

School integration was turning into a big issue by the 60s and 70s. Busing between schools to even up the black-white numbers was one way out. When Black faces appeared at my children's elementary school, my youngest daughter, a first-grader who had very fair skin and long blonde hair, suddenly stopped wanting to take baths. She wouldn't say why. After several days she tearfully confessed: "I'm too white!" At recess her new Black friends had teased her for that. But they were friends, and all was soon well. They went to each other's birthday parties.

All was not well with some parents of other kids at that school. They were especially upset at tales they heard about the school's one Black teacher. His name was Mr. Brown, and he taught 4th grade. I got phone calls from mothers:

"He makes them stand with their hands against the wall, just for talking in class!"

"My son says his arms hurt from holding them up so long!"
"He gives them too much homework!"

My son was in that class, and he had not bad-mouthed Mr. Brown. I told the outraged mothers to wait and see. At the end of that term there was an Awards Assembly. All of the classes and their teachers, and many parents (mostly the stay-at-home moms, since this was a daytime affair) gathered in the school auditorium. Class by class trooped in, each accompanied by their teacher, scrambled into rows of seats and sat down amid much giggling, scuffling and commotion. Mr. Brown's 4th-graders marched quietly in, took their places, and at a nod from him, all sat down at once. At awards time, each teacher took the podium and read off class accomplishments for Best Attendance, Best Speller, Best This, Best That. All of those teachers read from lists. When Mr. Brown took the stage, he had his hands in his pockets. He had no list. He grinned proudly at his students and called out the winners' names from memory, one after the other. On his birthday the girls in his class baked him a cake, and the boys made birthday cards. Bravo, Mr. Brown! I often wonder what became of him.

We all have school-day memories. What did we learn from them?

And what about the history most of us learned in school from first grade through high school?

To see how much history you remember, test your knowledge of what's true and not true. Try this quiz:

~

American History: True or False?

1. Columbus helped to bring slavery to the New World.

2. English colonists at Jamestown dug up corpses and ate them.

3. The "20 and odd Negroes" brought to Virginia in

1619 were not the only ones.

4. The Declaration of Independence had a section condemning slavery, but the Continental Congress took it out.

5. Thomas Jefferson and Sally Hemings had a family of mixed-race children.

6. The Constitution of the United States does not contain the word "slavery."

7. The Indian Removal Act forced 100,000 Native Americans off their lands—even though the Supreme Court ruled it was illegal.

8. Mexicans fought alongside Texans in defense of the Alamo.

9. A Women's Rights Convention in 1848 asked for the right to vote, but women did not get the vote until 1920.

10. Lincoln's Emancipation Proclamation did not end slavery.

~

Answers: Are you ready for this:? ALL of the above are <u>TRUE</u>.

If you got 10 out of 10 right, pat yourself on the back and give this book to a friend.

If you didn't get a perfect 10, keep reading and brace yourself. American history is not for the faint-hearted. It is a history of indomitable courage and unimaginable cruelty, of grit and greed, of want and wealth. It is also a history of ideas like liberty and equality and the pursuit of happiness—a history still very much in progress.

If we are ever to get it right, we need to know how we got here.

Forget the history you grew up with and try this version. Trust me. I'm not making this up. I've written two U.S. History textbooks and a bunch of other history books. You can look me up on Amazon: www.amazon.com/-/e/B001KCUZPC. I also helped write test questions for high school Advanced Placement American History exams. High school seniors pay to take them, and a good score can earn them college credits at most colleges and universities. (The AP Test Committee was told to avoid making up questions with "cultural bias," by not using words like "soul food" or "trust fund." What does that tell you?)

Not to worry, this book has no footnotes, and there is no exam at the end. But it will give you lots of things to think about, and maybe even talk about.

~

1. Columbus helped bring slavery to the New World.

Here's a verse you may remember from elementary school:

In fourteen hundred ninety-two
Columbus sailed the ocean blue.

You may not have learned the rest, but there's lots more to this poem written by a school teacher named Jean Marzollo in 1948.

He had three ships and left from Spain;
He sailed through sunshine, wind and rain.
He sailed by night; he sailed by day;
He used the stars to find his way.
A compass also helped him know

How to find the way to go.
Ninety sailors were on board;
Some men worked while others snored.
Then the workers went to sleep;
And others watched the ocean deep.
Day after day they looked for land;
They dreamed of trees and rocks and sand.
October 12 their dream came true,
You never saw a happier crew!

True, so far. So far, so good.

In 1492, when Columbus got here, he did not know that there were millions of people living in the Americas already: Some 12 to 16 million in Central and South America, another 5 million or more in North America. We don't know the exact numbers, but none of them was white.

Christopher Columbus never knew that in the vast mainland beyond island he landed on were the fabulous treasures of the Aztec and Inca empires. He never dreamed that their cities--Tenochitlán (now modern Mexico City) and the Inca capital at Cuzco, high in the Andes Mountains of Peru, were wealthy, sophisticated centers of commerce and culture in 1492. Before them, the Mayas had built a rich civilization from 300 to 900 A.D. in what is now Guatemala and the Yucatán peninsula. In North America the Mound Builders' huge earth pyramids and the Pueblos' multi-level adobe towns nourished vibrant societies. In the spring of 1607, around the time that Jamestown colonists arrived in Virginia, Mexico City was having a poetry festival.

Think about that, if you thought our ancestors were conquering a land full of ignorant savages.

"Indians! Indians!" Columbus cried;
His heart was filled with joyful pride.
But "India" the land was not;

In one of the worst mistakes ever made, Columbus pasted a label on a people who would have to live with it for the next five hundred years: The people he met were not "Indians." Later they would be called "Savages," "Red men," "American Indians," "Amerindians," "Native Americans," and "Indigenous Peoples." This last tactfully covers the natives of all the Americas. The Advanced Placement American History test question committees had to keep changing those names year after year. Same for "Negro." Once upon a time the polite (i.e. white) name was "colored." "Negro," in Columbus's day a perfectly good Spanish word meaning "black," was thought too near the N-word, which was rude and crude, except when used by black people to each other. Then came "people of color," "AfroAmericans," and finally "African Americans" or "Blacks." "Black is Beautiful" (that was the 1960s). Now, Black Lives Matter.

"Indian" is now a no-no word as well. Lots of sports teams that used to be called Redskins or Indians have changed their names. The Atlanta Braves have managed to keep theirs, maybe because they just won another World Series in 2021. The old cigar-store Indians, painted wooden figures seven feet tall, with feather war bonnets and tomahawks, are now collector's items worth big bucks. You won't see them outside your local tobacco shop. Statues have had a hard time of it, too. Teddy Roosevelt's statue, with TR on horseback, flanked by a Native American man and an African American man, both half-naked and on foot, has been moved west, from the American Museum of Natural History in New York City to the Theodore Roosevelt Presidential Library in Medora, North Dakota.

Back to Columbus and his "Indians": He thought he had reached India by sailing west to reach the east. This globe of earth was round, yes, but it was a good bit larger than people realized. Christopher Columbus made landfall in the Bahamas.

It was the Bahamas, and it was hot.
The Arakawa natives were very nice;
They gave the sailors food and spice.

In return, Columbus gave them smallpox and slavery.

Columbus brought diseases the "Indians" had never heard of, and neither had their immune systems: smallpox, measles, the plague, diphtheria, typhus, syphilis. These European bacteria and viruses killed the native peoples of the Americas by the untold millions. In a few decades the population of the New World was dramatically reduced by as much as 75 to 90 percent: too many deaths to count. Columbus also brought another contagious virus: the transatlantic slave trade. On his 1492 voyage Columbus took home seven Indians "to learn our language and return…or to be kept as captives." In almost no time, by 1503 a Spanish law allowed the enslavement of Caribbean natives. That was the beginning, the first link in the shackles that would bind millions of Africans. But Columbus and Spain and Portugal (these two nations had the same king until 1640) were not the only ones to blame.

In Africa, about which Europeans knew practically nothing, there were native kingdoms often at war with each other, and winners eager to sell their war captives for profit. With the help of African slave dealers, European traders were soon raking in huge profits, buying African men, women, and children to be sold as slaves in the New World. Marched to the coast in chains, loaded like cattle into the dark, stinking holds of ships, they endured the dreaded "Middle Passage," a 5,000-mile voyage from Africa to America . That would take nearly three months at sea, crowded together in a dark ship's hold most of the time, with a brief turn on deck now and then. Filth and death below. Some people said you could smell a slave ship long before you saw it. Conditions aboard these ships were so horrific that an English slave trader named John Newton felt guilty. He, repented of his sins, renewed his religious faith, and became a clergyman, pastor of a small church in England. There he wrote a hymn in 1779 called "Amazing Grace." That lovely classic (Who doesn't know at least the first verse by heart?) may be the only good thing to come out of the slave trade.

When I played a recording of "Amazing Grace" the first day of my graduate seminar on slavery, some of us got teary-eyed. The two African Americans in that class taught me something when I said I preferred the honest word "slave." to the new "enslaved people." They both said (and one of them was an elementary-school teacher), How would you feel if you were a black child in a classroom, and the teacher said your ancestors were slaves? 'Enslaved people' gives them some dignity. It shows that they were not responsible for what they were. I meekly agreed.

The transatlantic slave trade (or trade in enslaved people) began with hundreds, then thousands, then millions of human beings sold as chattel. That business, like the oil business in our own time fueled much of the global economy. The slave trade was the Exxon-Mobil of its day. Over the next 350 years the trade in human beings transported ten to fifteen million Africans to the Americas. None of them chose to come. About four to six million died on the way. Most wound up in South and Central America, but nearly four hundred thousand (some 388,000) of them were brought and sold in North America.

As far as we know, the first Africans in U.S. history set foot on Virginia soil. Virginia, founded in 1607, was the first of the original thirteen colonies, In a now-famous letter written In August 1619, a Virginia colonist named John Rolfe (the one who married Pocahontas) wrote that "20. and odd Negroes" had arrived on a Dutch ship. Because of the 1619 Project (begun in 2020 by the *New York Times*, a new look at our nation's history), we are getting a bigger picture. But historians of colonial America are contentious creatures (I know, being one myself), and *The 1619 Project: A New Origin Story* has stirred up a hornet's nest of criticisms from colonialists and others. Does American history begin with some Africans in Virginia in 1619? What about 1607 and Captain John Smith and Pocahontas at Jamestown? What about 1620 and the Pilgrims at Plymouth? Is slavery the main event of our earliest history?

In 1787, when the thirteen colonies became the United States of America, a nation of some 2,500,000 people, one fifth of them, or about 500,000, were enslaved Africans. Nobody argues about that.

Enslaved Africans helped build this country.

Their descendants are still here.

Do we owe them something?

~

2. English colonists at Jamestown dug up corpses and ate them.

Wait a minute, you say, where were John Smith and Pocahontas? Well, they were not there to see the cannibalism. Smith had sailed back to England in 1609, mysteriously and grievously wounded by a gunpowder explosion. (Did somebody there want to get rid of him? But that's another story.) Pocahontas, Powhatan's twelve-year-old daughter, came no more to turn cartwheels "naked as she was" around the English fort. By the way, Pocahontas and John Smith were never an Item. Do not believe the 1995 Walt Disney film, or the Terence Malick one of 2005.

Without Captain John Smith in the winter of 1609-10, English settlers huddled fearfully inside their log fort at Jamestown. The natives were hostile and the newcomers were hungry. The newcomers would soon be even hungrier. By the spring of 1610, of the three hundred English colonists inside the fort "not past sixty men, women, and children" were left alive. Many of the others had starved to death.

Some of the starving ones resorted to cannibalism.

They were driven *to doe those things which seame incredible, as to digge up deade corpes outt of graves and to eate them.*

--George Percy, "A Trewe Relacyon," 1624

Yes. One of the corpses they dug up was the body of a young English girl. Her skeleton has been excavated. There are knife marks where her skull was split open, and other knife marks on her leg bones. Someone wanted to eat her brains, her cheeks, and the flesh from her thigh bones. Those were the best parts.

Here is the back-story:

In the spring of 1607, 104 English men and boys set up housekeeping on the banks of a river they had named the "James" after their king, James I. The local Indians (about 14,000) called this river the "Powhatan," which was what they called their ruler. The newcomers and natives had made an uneasy peace with each other, but more newcomers kept coming, and the natives were feeling crowded. After John Smith left, the natives were angry, and the colonists were angry and hungry. To these English men and women, gnawing hunger was not only unfamiliar, it was unacceptable.

In seventeenth-century England, most people had enough to eat, however humble the fare. At home, even the poor had coarse bread or porridge, and now and then a chunk of cheese or morsel of meat. It was not fine fare, but it was filling. Outside the cities, ordinary people grew their own food and butchered their own meat. Workers in towns and cities often had meals given them as part of their wages. In London, "cook shops" sold meat pies, sausages, and other comestibles.

In Virginia, things were different. By the spring of 1610 the English at Jamestown were not only going to bed very hungry, they were slowly starving. All they had left to eat was half a can (a tin receptacle holding about four to eight ounces) of meal per person per day. For a modern comparison, one cup—eight ounces—of oatmeal has 300 calories. Adults need a minimum 1,500 to 2,000 calories per day to maintain a healthy body weight. Afraid of the Indians outside the fort, and rapidly running short of edibles inside the fort, what were these English settlers to do?

A colonist named George Percy wrote about the infamous "Starving Time":

Now all of us at James Towne beginneinge to feele the sharp pricke of hunger.... A world of miseries insued . . . we were gladd to make shifte with vermin, as doggs, Catts Ratts, and myce. . . . to eat Bootes shoes, or any other leather some could come by. And those being Spente and devoured, some were inforced to search the woodees and to feed upon Serpentts and snakes and to digge the earthe for wylde and unknowne Rootes. . . .
                    -George Percy, "A Trewe Relacyon," 1624

Yes. We have always known that Jamestown, the first permanent English settlement in America, was an ugly place, full of disease and death in the early years. That is why elementary school children learn about the Pilgrims who came to Plymouth, Massachusetts in 1620, as if they were the very first people here, and they had the first Thanksgiving. Not true: Spanish explorers near what is now El Paso, Texas held a Thanksgiving celebration on April 30, 1598. They were thankful that five hundred would-be colonists and 7,000 head of livestock had safely reached the Rio Grande River after a 50-day crossing of the Chihuahuan desert. After some prayerful feasting, they moved upriver and settled near what would become Santa Fe, New Mexico. That was the first Thanksgiving, but

Plymouth and the Pilgrims and the Indians and their turkeys have become icons in our national narrative.

In classrooms all over the U.S. first-graders color pictures of colonists in black and white clothes, and Indians with feather war bonnets (inaccurate, but colorful), and turkeys and pumpkins and ears of corn. Even with such a simple story, misconceptions can occur. When my mother taught first-graders in Center, Texas, in the 1930s, she asked them as they were leaving for the Thanksgiving holiday, "Now who can tell me again who the Pilgrims were?" A little boy's hand shot up. "Black and white people!"

We do not tell young children that before the Pilgrims came, many--no one knows exactly how many--of the English settlers at Jamestown starved to death, and that some of the starving ones dug up dead bodies and ate them. Thanks to the Jamestown Rediscovery Project's excavations, we now know that one of the corpses they ate was the body of a young English girl. No art work there for first-graders. That picture is scarier than any horror movie.

What do we tell the school children about cannibalism at Jamestown?

Few people know this today, but this nasty truth about the first permanent English colony was common knowledge in the 1600s:

The Indians hold the English surrounded...having killed the larger part of them...the survivors eat the dead....
                    --Alonso de Velasco to Philip III, June 14, 1610

(The Spanish ambassador loved to gloat over English failures.)

So great was our famine, that a savage we slew, and buried, the poorer sort took him up again and ate him, and so did diverse one another boiled and stewed with roots and herbs. -
                    -John Smith, Generall Historie, 1624

(Captain John Smith pulled no punches.)

[We were] *driven through unsufferable hunger unnaturally to eat those things which nature most abhorred: the flesh and excrements of man....as of our own nation as [well as] of an Indian digged by some out of his grave after he had lain buried three days, and wholly devoured him. Others, envying the better state of body of any whom hunger had not yet so much wasted as their own, lay [in] wait and threatened to kill and eat them.*

--"A Briefe Declaration...By the Ancient
Planters now remaining alive in Virginia," 1624.

(Some of the surviving colonists just wanted to tell the truth,)

Until now, many historians doubted these accounts, believing that those who wrote them had their own axes to grind:

George Percy, in command at Jamestown after a seriously injured John Smith returned to England, blamed Smith for not leaving enough food.

John Smith, when he wrote his history of Virginia, blamed George Percy's poor leadership.

Surviving Virginia colonists blamed the Virginia Company's mismanagement.

The Virginia Company said this was all fake news.

George Percy's narrative of starvation and desperation put in all the grisly details:

And some have Licked upp the Bloode which hathe fallen from their weake fellowes.

Percy left us with one other stomach-turning example of cannibalism at Jamestown:

. And amongst the reste this was moste lamentable. Thatt one of our Colline [colony] murdered his wife, ripped the Childe out of her woambe and threwe itt into the River, and after Chopped the Mother in pieces and sallted her for his foode.

If it makes you feel any better, the husband was executed for his crime.

~

3. The "20. and odd Negroes" brought to Virginia in 1619

were not the only ones.

>   *About the latter end of August* [1619], *a Dutch man of war of the burden of 160 tons arrived at Point Comfort, the commander's name Capt Jope, his pilot for the West Indies one Mr. Marmaduke an Englishman. They met with the Treasurer in the West Indies, and determined to hold consort . . . but in their passage lost one the other. He [Jope] brought not any thing but 20. And odd Negroes, which the governor and cape merchant bought . . . .Three or four days after [afterward] the Treasurer arrived . . . .*

Rolfe was not telling the whole story here. He failed to mention that the Treasurer also carried Africans.

The *Treasurer,* an old ship with a record of shady doings, stayed briefly at Point Comfort, nearly forty miles away at the James River's mouth.

"Before we got down," said Rolfe, the *Treasurer* "had set sail and was gone. . . ." Rolfe was not telling the whole truth here, either.

The *Treasurer* sailed from Virginia "in a very distressed state." The exact date is not known and the records are nonexistent, but there is reason to believe that the Treasurer, like the Dutch ship White Lion, also carried some captive Africans, and Virginians bought some of them. One of those Virginians was William Pierce [Rolfe's father-in-law, remember?]. Pierce later numbered among his servants "Angelo a Negro Woman in the Treasurer." She is listed in a census of 1625.

The 1625 census record shows that another planter, William Tucker, had in his household a young African couple, William and Isabel, and their child, William. There is unfortunately no record of the ship that brought them, or the date they arrived. But Tucker was commander at Point Comfort when the Treasurer stopped there in 1619. Since the Treasurer's last voyage to Virginia was in 1619—she was an old, decrepit ship and did not put to sea after 1620—William and Isabel, as well as Angelo were very likely on the Treasurer

Were these people slaves? Another sticky question

for historians, all of whom love to argue. Let us just say that slavery was illegal in England. The word slave was not related to race, as in Shakespeare's Hamlet saying, 'Oh, what a rogue and peasant slave am I." In the English colonies there were no laws about slaves or slavery until 1623 in Bermuda, and 1661 in Virginia. Both these English colonies, like others yet to be founded, had something called indentured servitude. Indentures, usually for seven years, bound a person to serve the one who bought his indenture. An indenture (so called because of the "indenture" made in the edges when the document was torn in pieces, one each to the parties involved.) An indenture was a contract: the owner promised to provide certain things—food, shelter, clothing, and usually a new suit and work tools at the end of service—to the servant, who promised to do as he or she was told in the service of said master.

Bermuda gave Africans indentures that were for 99 years. That, according to a legal-history expert friend of mine, was technically, legally not slavery. Who were they fooling?

Virginia did not use the word,"slavery" at first for the labor they got from African workers. Some of the earliest Africans worked off their indentures and a fortunate few, like one Anthony Johnson, acquired wives and children, and lived for a time as free people. Some of them even owned other Africans. For "one brief shining moment"(as the 1960 musical said of King Arthur's short-lived Camelot) Virginia was a place of hope and opportunity for Africans as well as English settlers. That story is told in other books, not this one. (The musical *Camelot* was a favorite of President John F. Kennedy's. That, too, is another story.)

However you want to split the hairs, it was not long until slavery soon became locked into law in the English colonies in North America, just as it was in the Spanish and Portuguese colonies in Central and South America.

The effects would be, and are, long-lasting.

~

4. The Declaration of Independence had a section condemning slavery, but it was deleted.

We hold these truths to be self-evident, that all men are created equal....

Thomas Jefferson wrote these words in 1776.

Nearly 250 years later, Americans are still struggling with their meaning:

Who are *"men"?*

What does *"equal"* mean?

At the time Jefferson wrote this, he owned at least 135 enslaved people. How could he not think of them, and the half a million other enslaved men, women, and children, in the thirteen American colonies? If he did think of them, he left no trace in his writings. Instead, Thomas Jefferson built his beloved plantation, Monticello, with some slave quarters hidden below the grassy turf, so as not to spoil the view from the house. Perhaps he did not want to be reminded of the people who cooked his food, washed his clothes, and made his bed. When Jefferson was composing the Declaration of Independence, did it occur to him that his slave valet, Robert Hemings, (more about the Hemingses later) might look over his shoulder and wonder what his master was writing?

In 1776, Thomas Jefferson, like many other American colonists, had other things besides slavery to worry about. They had had a serious falling-out with England, their mother country. They had protested the the Stamp Act in 1765 and argued bitterly about taxation (too much) and representation (too little) and their place in the British scheme of things. In 1768 they had seen British soldiers (Redcoats) pitching tents on Boston Common. In 1770 they had mourned when those very soldiers fired on a crowd of protesters and killed three (including a black sailor named Crispus Attucks) in what would go down in history as the Boston Massacre. Paul Revere made an engraving of it for a propaganda poster, showing soldiers firing their rifles at close range into the crowd, and red blood all over the ground. (If you find a copy of that poster today, you can sell it for a fortune and retire to the French Riviera.) In 1773 the colonists had been through the Boston Tea Party (that was the very first Tea Party, and like its namesake of 2009, it was full of hot-tempered people). In 1774 they had suffered under Parliament's Intolerable Acts (punishment for the Tea Party). Redcoats swarmed. Resentment and resistance were in the air. A Continental Congress met in Philadelphia to discuss all this, but little came of it. In 1775 the shooting began: After Paul Revere spurred his horse on a midnight ride to warn everyone that the British were coming, colonial militias (Minute Men) fought the battles of Lexington and Concord.

> *Here once the embattled farmers stood.*
> *And fired the shot heard round the world. . . .*

Ralph Waldo Emerson's 1837 poem, "Concord Bridge," has also been heard far and wide, but maybe not around the world.

Now, in the summer of 1776, American colonists were meeting again in Philadelphia, the City of Brotherly Love, for a second Congress. This time many of them thought things had gone far enough, and they were ready to cut their apron strings with England. In short, they wanted Independence. They appointed a "Committee of Five" to write a Declaration to that effect. Three of this group had names that every school child would learn: Benjamin Franklin. John Adams. Thomas Jefferson. The names of other two, Roger Sherman and Robert Livingston, escape most people. This Committee decided that Thomas Jefferson, being the youngest (he was 32) and some thought, the best writer of the lot, ought to do a draft document, and then the other four would get to criticize and edit.

On June 11, Jefferson began to write. No doubt he missed his wife, Martha, who was at home at Monticello. (There is a musical, *1776,* about this.) During Jefferson's stay in Philadelphia he was renting two upstairs rooms in a newly-built house at the southwest corner of Market and Seventh Streets. The owner, a bricklayer named Jacob Graff, had just finished his house the year before and was happy to rent out part of it. He sold it later, and in 1883 the house was torn down, and the Penn National Bank built a granite structure on that corner. In the 1960s, when I was a graduate student at the University of Pennsylvania, that corner was the home of the Tom Thumb Restaurant, with a sign that said,

CHEESEBURGERS ROOT BEER HOT DOGS

In 1975, in time for the Bicentennial of the American Revolution, this site became a tourist attraction. The Tom Thumb Restaurant was bulldozed, and a replica of the house where the Declaration of Independence was written was built as a historic site, which it is today.

In 1776 Thomas Jefferson had to steal time to write, since he was also attending all-day sessions of the Continental Congress as a delegate from Virginia. Unfortunately, neither he nor his fellow committee members kept notes about the next seventeen days and nights of composing what would be one of the most famous documents in the world.

When Jefferson finished his work, it included this paragraph on slavery:

He [King George] *has waged cruel war against human nature itself, violating its most sacred rights of life and liberty in the persons of a distant people who never offended him, captivating & carrying them into slavery in another hemisphere or to incur miserable death in their transportation thither. This piratical warfare, the opprobrium of infidel powers, is the warfare of the Christian King of Great Britain. Determined to keep open a market where Men should be bought & sold, he has prostituted his negative for suppressing every legislative attempt to prohibit or restrain this execrable commerce. . . .*

When Jefferson finished the whole draft, he showed it first to John
Adams, who later wrote about it in his diary:

I was delighted with its high tone and the flights of oratory with which it abounded, especially that concerning Negro slavery, which, though I knew his Southern brethren would never suffer to pass in Congress, I certainly never would oppose . . . .

John Adams was for it, but Southerners, as you might guess, were not.

On June 28 Jefferson and the other four committee members had a finished product ready to present to the Congress for its approval. All the delegates would have a chance to criticize it. When that happened, the Continental Congress, sitting as a Committee of the Whole, decided to cut out the entire paragraph on slavery.

A disappointed Jefferson made note of this:

The clause . . . reprobating the enslaving the inhabitants of Africa, was struck out in compliance to South Carolina and Georgia, who had never attempted to restrain the importation of slaves, and who on the contrary still wished to continue it. Our Northern brethren also I believe felt a little tender under these censures; for tho' their people have very few slaves themselves yet they had been pretty considerable carriers of them to others.

—Thomas Jefferson,"
Notes of Proceedings in Congress."

Nobody in 1776 wanted to touch what was already a touchy subject. They would tiptoe around it again in 1787 when they drafted the Constitution. (More about that later in Number 5 below.) Slavery, the biggest skeleton in the American closet, would not be buried until 1865. (That was not the Emancipation Proclamation (see Number 9 below.)

Slavery ended, but its legacy did not. It lingers to this very day.

"Slavery continues to play a part in American life, as Americans discover that their national buildings were constructed by slaves, their great cities are underlaid with the bones of slaves, and their greatest heroes and heroines were slaveowners and slaves. Coming to terms with slavery's complex history is no easier in the twenty-first century than it was in centuries past.

--Ira Berlin, *Generations of Captivity:*
A History of African-American Slaves (2003),
14-15.

"If we're going to be a country that feels like Jefferson is important and Washington is important and the Declaration of Independence is important, and we're going to be patriotic on July 4, then we have to be the same way about the things that shame us. . . . Either the past matters or it doesn't."
—Ta-Nehisi Coates, *The New York Times,*
June 19, 2019.

"Yet the defense of slavery was deeply shaken in theory by the Revolution's egalitarian principle, and the institution of slavery was shaken in practice when blacks took advantage of the disruptions of the war. . . . This contradiction is at the heart of the story of the founding of the United States. It raises questions that remain central to how democracy and equality are experienced in the present. The current discussion of reparations for slavery is an example of this . . . .
--Linda Kerber, May 30, 2000,
excerpt from the author's US history textbook.

That was in 2000. We are still discussing.

~

5. Thomas Jefferson and Sally Hemings had a family of mixed-race children.

Another touchy subject. Unless you have been under a rock for the past several decades, you know about Jefferson and Sally. How could a Founding Father father children by an enslaved woman? Many people refuse to believe that to this very day. There was a time when eminent Jefferson scholars also pooh-poohed the Jefferson-Hemings story. Some Jefferson experts even tried to bury it. A television series based on a novel about it never reached the networks. But by the 1990s diligent research including DNA studies and prizewinning books pretty well proved it.

Long before that, here is what I used to tell my students: Let the circumstantial evidence speak for itself. When Thomas Jefferson married Martha Wayles Skelton in 1771, he was twenty-seven, and she was twenty-two. They were very much in love. She bore him seven children, but only two daughters lived to adulthood. When Martha died of complications after the birth of their last child in

1782, Jefferson was out of his mind with grief. On her deathbed, Martha made him promise never to marry again, and of coursed he promised. Servants talk. One of the people who no doubt heard about that sad vow was a young slave girl in Jefferson's household, Sally Hemings, age nine.

Sally's father was a white Virginia planter, John Wayles, and her mother was a mixed-race slave, Betty Hemings. Note: Jefferson's slave valet, Robert Hemings (see Number 4 above) was Sally's brother. Sally's grandfather was a white sea captain. Her grandmother was a slave. Sally was a very light-skinned quadroon— that is, she was one-quarter black.

Sally Hemings and Martha Wayles Jefferson had the same father: John Wayles. They were half-sisters.

There are no pictures of Sally, and none of Martha, but hearsay has it that they resembled each other—and that they were both comely young women. There are no letters from Sally. We don't even know if she could write. There are no letters from Martha, because Jefferson burned them.

The story of Thomas Jefferson and Sally Hemings begins in 1785, when he was the new United States ambassador to France. He took his eldest daughter Martha, age fifteen, with him, but left his two younger daughters in Virginia. Then Lucy, the youngest, died of whooping cough, and Jefferson decided to send for her sister Maria (Polly) age nine, to join him and her older sister Martha in Paris. Because an older woman servant took sick and could not make the trip, Sally Hemings, now fourteen, was the one who accompanied Polly on the long, dangerous transatlantic crossing.

Abigail Adams, John's wife, living in London while John was ambassador to England (1785-1788), met the two girls, and wrote to Jefferson. Abigail was worried. Sally Hemings, a pretty teenager, was going to live in Paris with Thomas Jefferson, a widower, age 42. Sally may have looked a lot like her half-sister, Jefferson's beloved late wife.

If you saw the 1995 James Ivory film, "Jefferson in Paris," you know what happened next. But neither James Ivory nor anyone else can get at the truth.

What we do know is that when Thomas Jefferson and his entourage returned to America in 1789, Sally Hemings was pregnant. That child, born at Monticello in 1790, "lived but a short time."

In the next nineteen years, Sally Hemings would bear six more children —all of them very likely fathered by Thomas Jefferson. Every time Jefferson, (who was busy being Secretary of State, Vice President, and then President) spent time at Monticello, Sally Hemings gave birth nine months later. Four of these infants, three sons and a daughter, lived to adulthood.

This story got into print in 1802, when one of [then President] Jefferson's political enemies, a journalist, started spreading a scandal (does that sound familiar?). He wrote that Jefferson had a slave mistress who had birthed "a litter" of children by him. Anti-Jefferson newspaper articles about this were vulgar, gutter-level racism, with references to "Sooty Sally" and her light-skinned son, "President Tom." Some of these stories would never make it into print today, even in the tabloids. Jefferson chose to ignore them all—but he never denied them. His political enemies loved it. Was it true?

In those days, people who visited Monticello, Jefferson's Virginia home, sometimes remarked upon various young enslaved servants' resemblance to Jefferson. Four of Sally's children lived to be grown-ups, and all of them became free: two were runaways, never pursued, and Jefferson's will freed the two younger sons. After Jefferson's death in 1825, his daughter Martha gave Sally her freedom. Sally Hemings spent her last years in Charlottesville, Virginia, with her sons Madison and Eston. She died in 1835. No one knows to this day where she was buried.

In 1873 Sally's son Madison, then living in Ohio, revealed to a journalist the story his mother had told him long ago: he and his siblings were Thomas Jefferson's children. Madison Hemings's story was a bombshell. It was so sensational and shocking that few people believed it.

Until the late 20th century, most historians, including distinguished Jefferson scholars, didn't buy the Hemings story, either, and said so. But in 1997, with the advent of DNA technology, tests of the chromosomes of male descendants of Jeffersons and Hemingses pointed out their connections. By now, the poignant story of Sally Hemings, the young enslaved girl who reminded Jefferson of his wife, and who bore Jefferson's children, who lived with him and cared for him until his death in 1825 is accepted as true—by most people. Annette Gordon Reed tells the whole story in her 2009 prize-winning book, *The Hemingses of Monticello: An American Family.*

Did Thomas Jefferson and Sally Hemings love each other? We will never know. When I visited Monticello in 1975 there was an exhibit of some of Jefferson's personal items, like his notebook for records of expenses, and, oddly enough, samples of his under-drawers and handkerchiefs. They were fine, white cotton, and each piece had a tiny number, from 1 to 13, exquisitely embroidered in white near the hem. Speculation was that the meticulous, fastidious Jefferson wanted to be sure he wore them in order. No one really knew what those numbers meant, I stood before that glass case a long time, imagining Sally Hemings sitting in a chair, lovingly, painstakingly, stitching "*1,*" "*2,*" "*3. . . .*"

~

6. The Constitution of the United States does not contain the word, "slavery."

When my U.S. History class got to the Constitution, I used to look out the classroom window and say, 'If we went outside right now and asked three passers-by on Mt. Vernon Street (yes, that was its name) if *We, the People* begins the Declaration of Independence, two out of the three would say yes. Would they be right?" There was usually a pause, as students wondered if this was a trick question. That was before smart phones, so nobody could surreptitiously Google it. Then someone who peeked at the textbook would say, No. The Declaration begins, *We hold these truths . . . .*" and "*We, the People"* begins the Constitution.

Then I would launch into a little sermon about the Declaration and the Constitution being our founding documents, and how we all should know and remember what's in them. If I were teaching that class today, I'd probably start with, "How many of you have seen "Hamilton"? But back then, I began with the back story: who wrote the Constitution? For now, that's as good a place as any, if we want to think about slavery and the infamous Three-Fifths Clause.

For starters, all of the "People" who wrote the United States Constitution were white males. (What did I tell you at the beginning of this book—most of US. history up to now has been written by white males. Our Constitution, likewise.) There were fifty-five of them. They were a youthful lot. Four of them were in their twenties. Alexander Hamilton was just thirty. Another thirteen were just a little older, still in their thirties. James Madison was thirty-six. Nearly half of them, of them, twenty-three to be exact, were in their forties. George Washington, the chair of the convention, was fifty-five. He was already a national hero from the Revolutionary War, with songs written about him, and babies named after him. Benjamin Franklin was the oldest delegate, at eighty-one. Roger Sherman (remember him from the Declaration of Independence committee?) was sixty-six. In case you are wondering, the other members of that Declaration committee—Thomas Jefferson, John Adams, and Robert Livingston—were not part of the Constitutional Convention. Jefferson, you may remember, was in Paris; Adams, in London, and Livingston was Chancellor of New York at the time.

The drafters of the Constitution were a well-educated lot, with thirty-one college degrees among them. They were also well off financially. They had to be, since they were writing the Constitution and living in Philadelphia and paying expenses out of their own pockets. A dozen were lawyers, and another dozen (remember this) were planters. As one historian later wrote of them, these fifty-five white males were a convention of "the well-bred, the well-fed, the well-read, the well-bred, and the well-wed." About one-third of them held enslaved people (keep this in mind). The historian was the late distinguished James MacGregor Burns, and his 1982 book was *the Vineyard of Liberty.*

Liberty is not a word much used these days. The Massachusetts Puritan John Winthrop (who coined the description of his colony as a "city upon a hill") said in 1645 that there are two kinds of liberty, "natural," to do as you please, and "civil," to do only that which is "good, just, and honest."

The Virginia lawyer Patrick Henry in 1775 said "Give me liberty . . . . " (If you don't know the rest, I'm not going to tell you.)

A cracked bell hanging in Independence National Park in Philadelphia bears its name.

A towering statue in New York harbor carries its torch.

Liberty has to do with freedom, and with power. Who has it?

These days, anti-maskers clash with mask-wearers, anti-vaxxers with the vaccinated. Democrats clash with Republicans. Proud Boys and QAnon and Oath Keepers clash with--- let's not go there.

Back to the Constitution and the slavery issue. We skip over all of the Convention's long (tedious to us, but of vital interest to them) debates over representation, state powers, the presidency. I used to give my students a mnemonic for the topics of the seven articles of the United States Constitution:

Children Eat Jelly Sandwiches And Seafood Regularly.

When I wrote those words on the blackboard and turned around, I faced a forest of puzzled faces. Nobody ever got it. I always had to explain: "C," I would say, stands for Congress, E, for Executive," and so on: Judicial, States, Amendments, Supremacy, Ratification. Some of my students may still remember. I hope so. You might find them handy, yourself.

We now fast-forward over debates on the powers of Congress, the states, and the President. I used to tell my students that Alexander Hamilton wanted the President to be like a king, to serve for life. Hamilton also wanted a Senate appointed for life, and only the House of Representatives elected by popular vote. (Lin-Manuel Miranda's Hamilton danced around those.)

Our fifty-five delegates began their official deliberations on a rainy Friday morning in Philadelphia, May 25, 1787. They met in Independence Hall, where some of them had been before in 1776, when they voted for—you guessed it. Now they would meet there again, until September 17. They spent a long, hot summer with no air conditioning. We hope they took off their coats and unbuttoned their waistcoats, but we don't know. Manners and dress codes were more formal in those days. They kept the doors closed, and the shades down. The public was definitely not allowed in. Some people thought the whole thing was a conspiracy. (Yes, we had conspiracy theories even then.)

The Convention did not get around to the "three-fifths" clause until August 29. That clause has to do with counting a population for representation and taxation: voting (as we know all too well these days) and paying taxes are two key items that make democracy work. Then construction on the ship of state these men were building came to a halt. Representation was the problem. How do you do a head count when one out of every six heads is an enslaved one? (Note: this one-out-of-six figure is based on the first U.S. Census, taken in 1790. At that time total population was nearly 4,000,000, which included 700,000 slaves. Do the math.)

How serious was this problem? So serious that the United States Constitution did not dare to mention the word, *slavery,* let alone, *slaves.* I used to have my students look for those words in their textbook copies of the document, and they were always surprised not to find them. Then I referred them to this passage right up there on the first page of the Constitution in Article I:

Section 2: The House of Representatives:Representatives and direct Taxes shall be apportioned among the several States which may be included within this Union, according to their respective Numbers, which shall be determined by adding to the whole Number of free Persons, including those bound to Service for a Term of Years, and excluding Indians not taxed, three fifths of all other Persons.

For the makers of the Constitution, there were "free Persons" and "other Persons." Who were they kidding? More to the point, why were they skirting, dancing around, putting lipstick on the pig of an ugly truth?

Every man in that convention knew that they had just created a nation with a Declaration of Independence that said, *All men are created equal, that they are endowed by their Creator with certain unalienable Rights, that among these are Life, Liberty and the pursuit of Happiness.*

Every man sweating through endless debates on those hot summer days knew how this argument would end. The men from the slave states would win, just as they had won the debate over deleting the slavery paragraph in the Declaration of Independence. If this new-born nation were to survive, its fragile body had to be made of the slave states as well as the free. Everybody in that convention hall knew that. Then the delegates ran into another hard question: if an enslaved person cannot vote, how can he be a "Person" counted in a state's population to determine its number of representatives in Congress?

Roger Sherman said that a state's total population (he was from Connecticut, a small state) should determine its representation in Congress, and that was that. Charles Pinckney (he was from South Carolina, a big slave state) agreed absolutely. But Gouverneur

Morris of Pennsylvania (he was from a big state without much slavery) argued that to count an enslaved person as a full person would encourage the South to keep up the slave trade. The vessel they were trying to launch had run into a rock, but they refused to give up: If not "Person," then how about a fraction of a person?

One-half of a person, said one.

What about three-fourths, said another.

Charles Pinckney's suggestion of three-fifths of a person finally won the day. James Madison and Edmund Randolph (both from Virginia, another big slave state) opposed this. They wanted to count each enslaved person as a whole person. How come? Do the numbers. If slave states got to count their enslaved as whole persons, they would get more seats in the House of Representatives, which bases its number of representatives on a state's population. (Senators, I hope you know, are even-steven: two from each state, period. This plan was to suit the needs of a new nation more than two and a half centuries ago. It does not work well for us now. Think about this.) In 1787, even with the 3/5 compromise, counting every enslaved person as three-fifths of a person gave the states with more enslaved persons, i.e., the South, a built-in political advantage.

I used to tell my students to remember that, as we forged ahead to the end of the semester and the Civil War, when all enslaved 3/5 persons were free and suddenly counted as whole persons. And what about Reconstruction, when those former enslaved persons got to vote? Most would join the Republican Party, the party founded back in 1854 in order to oppose slavery. (The Republican Party of the 21st century is an entirely different animal.)

The Constitutional Convention of 1787 did not finish the whole document until September 17, when they adjourned after signing it. Only thirty-seven of the fifty-five signed. Three refused. Others found reasons to go home. Rhode Island, the smallest state, had never bothered to come. But Gouverneur Morris cleverly worded the form:

Done in Convention, by the unanimous consent of the States present the 17 September.

While the signing was in progress, Benjamin Franklin made a comment worth quoting here. He said he had often looked at the back of George Washington's chair, which had a sunrise painted on it. In the course of the summer, he said, "I have looked at that behind the President without being able to tell whether it was rising or setting. But now I have the happiness to know that it is a rising and not a setting sun."

Let's hope he was right.

~

7. The Indian Removal Act forced 100,000 Native Americans off their lands—even though the Supreme Court ruled it was illegal.

Chickasaw. Choctaw. Potowatomi. Creek. Sauk. Fox. Seminole. Cherokee. In the 1830s, over a hundred thousand of them—men, women, and children—had to leave their tribal homelands in the eastern United States and move west to a land none of them had ever seen. Thousands died on the journey. Part of it is known to this day as the Trail of Tears.

For many years, white Americans had been wanting to get rid of the Indians who still lived on land the Indians thought was theirs. But the new American settlements needed more room. How were they to get it without getting scalped? Whites plotted to move eastern Indians to the Far West—in those days that meant west of the Mississippi River. That was Indian Country. That was one reason for the Louisiana Purchase, back in 1803. It opened up a place to put the Indians.

President Thomas Jefferson, who presided over the Louisiana Purchase, had long favored moving the Indians out west. When Andrew Jackson was elected president in 1828, he favored it even more. The United States was growing fast. Since George Washington had presided over a nation of thirteen states, eleven new states had joined the Union. (In case you are wondering, these were Vermont, Kentucky, Tennessee, Ohio, Louisiana, Indiana, Mississippi, Illinois, Alabama, Maine, and Missouri.) White Americans needed more and more land. They viewed the Indians as unlettered savages, and the Indians viewed the whites as greedy land-grabbers. Both sides got it partially right.

President Jackson, an old Indian fighter himself, feared violence between Indians and whites would come soon unless something was done. That something was the Indian Removal Act of 1830. It was designed to move the "aborigines" to a place of safety where they could learn "the arts of civilization." Civilization? The Cherokee Nation in Georgia already had a written alphabet in their native language, devised by a Cherokee named Sequoyah. (Yes, the giant evergreen trees in California were named "sequoias" after him.) With their alphabet, Cherokees had become better at reading and writing than many of their white Georgia neighbors. Cherokees had a government that did not exclude women, even on war councils. Their Cherokee language newspaper, the *Cherokee Phoenix,* spoke out against the Indian Removal Act. Fifteen thousand Cherokees petitioned Congress against it, but these "uncivilized" people had to leave, anyway. The Supreme Court of the United States, in *Worcester v. Georgia,* ruled that the Indian Removal Act was unconstitutional. But President Andrew Jackson supposedly said that Chief Justice Marshall "has made his decision. Now let him enforce it." That was Andrew Jackson, for you. (Does he remind you of any other president?)

Jackson ordered Indian Removal, and he got his way. For starters, U.S. soldiers rounded up 13,000 Cherokees from their homes in Georgia and stuffed them into hastily-built stockades. Families--men, women, children--were penned up for months in squalid surroundings, where they suffered overcrowding, illness, and despair. (Does this sound familiar?) Three to four thousand Cherokees died, either in the stockades or on the "Trail of Tears" as they made their way over the 1,000 miles from Georgia to Indian Territory (now Oklahoma) in 1838.

Some Indians fought back: In 1832 in Illinois, Chief Black Hawk led members of the Sauk and Fox tribes against U.S. troops and state militia in the Black Hawk War. One of those U.S. soldiers was a twenty-three-year-old militia volunteer named Abraham Lincoln. He never saw action, saying later that the only blood he saw was from mosquito bites. There was plenty of action elsewhere: In the Bad Axe Massacre (fought near the aptly named Bad Axe River), U.S. forces killed between 400 and 500 Sauk and Fox men, women, and children.

In Florida the Seminole War of 1835-1838 was even bloodier, with guerrilla raids by the Indians led by Chief Osceola. They put up a good fight, 3,000 of them against nearly 30,000 U.S. soldiers. But Chief Osceola was captured and died in prison in 1838, and the Seminoles finally gave up. Nearly 4,000 of them wound up in Indian Territory, but others hunkered down in Florida and refused to leave. Some of them still live there. The Choctaws, about 15,000 of them, were driven out of their homes in Alabama, Mississippi, Arkansas, and Louisiana in the dead of winter and forced to walk to Indian Territory. About 2,500 of them died on the way. Several hundred Potowatomis were forced off their lands in Indiana "marching in a line, surrounded by soldiers who were hurrying their steps. Next came the baggage wagons, in which numerous invalids, children, and women, too weak to walk, were crammed." This "Trail of Death," a 660-mile trek to Indian Territory in what is now Kansas, killed over 40 Native Americans, mostly children.

This story does not end in here. The troubled, tangled history of relations between Native Americans and the government of the United States is well treated in books much larger than this one.

I used to tell my students one story with a good ending: In 1637 the Pequot War in Connecticut killed hundreds of Pequot men, women, and children, many of whom died at sunrise one horrible day when colonial militiamen surprised their village and burned it to the ground. In 1998 (361 years later) the Mashantucket Pequot Museum and Research Center opened in Mashantucket, Connecticut. This museum recounts the Pequot tribe's history in stunning exhibits that include a full-size re-creation of a Pequot village. Life-like figures (no plastic, real fur, real deerskin) demand attention. As a matter of fact, so do items in the museum shop: a miniature ceremonial rattle made of wood and deerskin and feathers, a pair of earrings made from purple and white quahog shells. I know, because I bought these items. How did the Pequots have the money to create this extraordinary, expensive museum? The answer, in a word, is— gambling.

Native Americans on tribal lands can play by their own rules, as long as they do not violate any federal laws. The U.S. federal government has always recognized Native American tribal lands as separate entities, treating them as sovereign states, as it were, a state within a state. Native Americans—then called Indians—are in the Constitution:

Article I, Section 2 says that representation and taxation are apportioned among the states, "excluding Indians not taxed."

Article I, Section 8 say that Congress has power to regulate commerce with foreign nations, among the state, "and with the Indian tribes."

Native Americans on tribal lands can gamble. That means they can have casinos in states where gambling is forbidden. Guess who flocks to these casinos with pockets full of cash? Right: People from places where gambling is illegal. Now 240 Native American tribes operate some 460 casinos scattered across the U.S. Some—the Pequots being the best example—have been more successful than others. Some have gone bankrupt.

As for the Pequots, they opened a bingo hall on their reservation in 1986, then the Foxwood Casino in 1992, and made a fortune. Over the years, that meant billions of dollars. Members of the Pequot tribe could afford the best of everything. They could travel anywhere they liked. Ivy League colleges wooed their children, who could pay full tuition. Since then, there have been some ups and downs, but today Foxwood Resort and Casino remains one of the largest casinos in the United States. That, I used to tell my students, is the Pequot revenge for what happened to them in 1637.

What happened to America's Native Americans under federal laws? Here, for the record:

In 1887 the Dawes Act divided Indian reservations into individual plots of land, not to be sold for 25 years. Indian families who registered with the federal government got 160 acres to farm, or 320 acres of grazing land. President Grover (the Good) Cleveland signed this act and thought it a fine thing. After all, President Abraham Lincoln had signed a Homestead Act in 1862, giving 160 acres of free land to any citizen who registered and promised to "homestead," to build a home and farm the land. Now the Dawes Act was extending the same privilege to Indians.

Whoa! The Dawes Act was giving back to Indians land they already possessed. It was carving up their reservations into little farms. The only hitch was, Indians were not farmers. They lived in tribal communities. They shared what they grew. They hunted and fished. They were not interested in becoming farmers. The Dawes Act was not a great success.

In 1903 the US Supreme Court ruled that Congress could dispose of Indian lands without Indians' consent. Indian-owned lands in 1887 were 154 million acres, 50 years later, Indian-owned lands had shrunk to 48 million acres.

In 1924 the Citizenship Act made all Native Americans citizens of the United States of America. About time.

In 1934 the Indian Reorganization Act reversed the Dawes Act and gave back un-allotted Indian lands to the control of Native American tribes.

That is far from the end of the story. David Grann's *Killers of the Flower Moon,* a recent best-selling book about what happened in one Oklahoma town tells a harrowing tale: Many Osage Indians in Pawhuska, Oklahoma, not only lost their oil-rich land to unscrupulous whites; many of them were secretly murdered for it. We did not know that when my family lived in Pawhuska in 1948. It was a pretty little town, hilly, and with what seemed to us a large number of big houses. We were told that the imposing mansions now for sale or rent had once belonged to "Indians who got rich on oil money, built big houses, squandered their money, and went broke." We rented one of those mansions—the grandest house we ever lived in: a large white edifice with a two-story wrap-around porch, four bedrooms upstairs, a bathroom big enough to play handball in; a sun room, a library, and a cavernous living room and dining room. I remember the bitterly cold winter we spent there, when the temperature outside often dipped way below zero. Floor furnaces in that big, drafty house could not keep us warm. We closed off the living room and dining room with their elegant panelling and pocket doors and lived mostly in the kitchen. My best friend in the sixth grade was an Osage Indian girl whose family lived in a little frame house on the Osage Reservation. I sometimes spent the night with her, but she did not want to sleep at my house.

~

8. Mexicans fought alongside Texans in defense of the Alamo.

Like American history, Texas history is full of myths. The Battle of the Alamo is a giant one with several parts. It goes something like this: In 1836 a brave band of 187 Anglo "Texians" inside an old Spanish mission in San Antonio fought to their deaths against an invading army of 4,000 Mexicans led by the villainous General Antonio López de Santa Anna. The Texians were fighting to keep Texas free from tyranny. They were defending democracy. The defenders of the Alamo refused to surrender. They fought bravely and died to the last man. This heroic battle became world-famous, and of course, all Texas school children learned it. Texas History was a required subject in the seventh grade.

I was in Oklahoma in the seventh grade, and as far as I can recall, we did not study Oklahoma History. I learned about the Alamo from my father, on a family trip to San Antonio when I was seven years old. He led me by the hand through the old mission church, speaking in reverent tones, reading to me from the copy of Colonel William B. Travis's famous letter of February 24, 1836: *I shall never surrender or retreat.* My father told me the story of how Travis drew a line in the dirt and asked all who wanted to stay and fight, to step across the line. He told me the story of how Jim Bowie, lying ill on a cot, asked for his bed to be carried across that line. He told me how Davy Crockett of Tennessee had fought bravely and died for Texas. My father was born and bred in Illinois, but he knew all about the Alamo. Its mythical history is known far and wide.

In 1991 my husband was involved with the Kennedy Center Texas Festival, and, despite his tactful suggestions, the opening night reception in Washington D.C. at the Kennedy Center featured a huge papier maché replica of –you guessed it—the Alamo. That iconic facade, which someone said resembles a Dutch headboard, is familiar world-wide. The original church at the old mission did not look anything like it. And most of the battle of the Alamo was fought in and around the Long Barracks, not the church. That's the power of a myth.

On April 21, 1836, not long after the March 6 battle of the Alamo, Sam Houston and his Texans trounced Santa Ana and his Mexicans at the Battle of San Jacinto, shouting "Remember the Alamo."

In 1845 Texas was admitted to the Union as the twenty-eighth state, with slaves. It had a majority of Anglo-Texans, many of whom harbored a lasting and virulent ill will toward Mexicans.

That reminds me of a story one of my former students told me when she first taught a room full of seventh-graders about the Alamo.

"I looked out at those faces—three-fourths of them Hispanics—and I thought, What am I doing to say to these kids? How can I get this Alamo story across? Then I happened to look out the window on the athletic field, and I saw a big pile of cardboard cartons waiting for the trash. Put down your books, and come outside, I told the class. They were puzzled, but they did as I asked. Now, I said, See that pile of boxes? Well, you are going to build the Alamo with them—and when you are done, you have to decide if you want to be inside it as a defender or outside it as an attacker!" She said her brainstorm worked: about half the Hispanics got inside, along with the white kids, and the others, whooping and hollering, attacked.

"When the battle was over, we went back inside and had a really good discussion about who was who, and who was 'right' and who was 'wrong.'"

To this day, the Texas Education Agency has ongoing problems with textbooks and teaching Mexican-American history in schools. Some myths are hard to let go.

To get the story right, there were Mexicans among the "Texians" inside the Alamo, at least nine of them, fighting alongside Anglos, shooting at Mexicans outside in Santa Anna's army. "Mexicanos" in short, were on both sides.

For example, in April 1835 a twenty-nine-year-old Mexican named Juan Nepomuceno Seguin joined Stephen F. Austin's "Army of the People" to fight against Mexico's autocratic rule over Texas. A year later Juan Seguin would be one of the band of rebels defending the Alamo against Santa Anna's troops. Because Seguin spoke Spanish, he was assigned to slip through the Mexican lines to carry word of the Alamo's plight, and by the time he returned, the battle of the Alamo was over. He had missed all the excitement. In 1837, when the ashes of the Alamo dead were laid to rest in San Antonio, it was Lieutenant Colonel Juan Seguin who delivered the eulogy. He went on to serve as a senator in the Congress of the Republic of Texas, and in 1841 and '42, as mayor of San Antonio. Juan Seguin did not speak or write a word of English. A Texas city is named for him.

Three of the fifty-nine signers of the Texas Declaration of Independence were Mexicans. One of them, Lorenzo de Zavala, would be the first vice-president of the new Republic of Texas.

That pretty well disposes Myth #1, that brave Anglos fought to defend the Alamo against dastardly Mexican attackers. But there are other Alamo myths. Historians love to argue, and no Texas history conference can do without a session or two on the Alamo. The 2021 book mentioned earlier, *Forget the Alamo*, by Burrough, Tomlinson, and Stanford, will no doubt take its place in conferences to come. The authors present some unwelcome additions to the Alamo story, the main one being that the hero-defenders were fighting to keep slavery. Mexico had abolished slavery in 1829, five years earlier. What Texans said and did about that is a tale too long to put into this book. It tarnishes the shining images of people like Stephen F. Austin, who asked Mexico to help Texans keep their slaves, and Jim Bowie, who, besides being a good drinker and a pretty fair knife fighter, was a slave trader. There are other myths now in disfavor: Travis probably never drew a line in the dirt. Davy Crockett did not die fighting. Many people forget that Sam Houston ordered the defenders to abandon the Alamo, to get out before the Santa Anna's army got there, and they chose to disobey those orders. But the Alamo story as a time-hallowed Big Myth is likely to be around for years to come. There are differing visions of what the reimagined Alamo museum, supposed to open in 2025, will be.

Different visions of the Alamo set off the epic feud between the two factions of the Daughters of the Republic of Texas, led by Adina de Zavala (granddaughter of Lorenzo de Zavala) and Clara Driscoll (granddaughter of Daniel O'Driscoll, who fought at the Battle of San Jacinto) began in the early 1900s and went on for years. Each of these formidable women held different views of the Alamo and its preservation. De Zavala once barricaded herself in the Alamo for three days. She wanted to preserve a structure known as the Long Barracks, where much of the actual battle of the Alamo took place: Driscoll disagreed. Their story is too long to include here, but the battle of the Alamo did not die with Adina and Clara. The DRT was a formidable force, in charge of the Alamo for a hundred years.

One example, from personal experience: In the 1990s, when the U.S. History Advanced Placement Exam readings were held at Trinity University in San Antonio, many historians, who came from all over the United States, had never seen the Alamo. Since we readers had to work grading exams from 9 to 5 every day, and the Alamo closed at 5 o'clock every day, our Chief Reader sent a special request to the DRT to stay open after 5 one day so the historians could visit. The answer was a polite but no-nonsense "No." Despite subsequent pleas from the president of Trinity University and other prominent officials, the unbending DRT still answered no.

This organization remains a formidable group even today, although the DRT is no longer in charge of the Alamo. In 2016 the Texas General Land Office took over that job.

"Remember the Alamo," indeed.

~

9. American women did not ask for the right to vote until 1848, and they did not get it until 1920.

In 1848, more than sixty years after the founding of the United States of America, women made up nearly half the population of the new nation, but they were, as one of them put it, "civilly dead." A woman could not vote, or hold public office (much less speak in public before a mixed audience for fear it would "unsex" her). Most colleges did not admit women. Heaven help the woman who dreamed of becoming a minister or a lawyer or a doctor. Women were delicate creatures fit only to be wives and mothers. Women had no heads for figures, no business running a business. A married woman had little or no control over her property or income. It she earned money, it belonged to her husband. Unless she signed a prenuptial agreement, what was his was his, and what was hers was his, too. Divorce was a disgrace too awful to mention, and a failed marriage was nearly always blamed on the wife. Husbands usually got custody of the children. In almost every state, wife-beating "with a reasonable instrument" was legal as late as 1850.

Thanks largely to the efforts of two white women who set things in motion, all this was about to change.

Elizabeth Cady Stanton (1815-1902) grew up in Johnstown, New York, knowing that her father wished she had been a boy. Judge Daniel Cady and his wife had five sons, and all of them had died. Nothing Elizabeth could do to please her father made up for that. She studied Greek; she learned to ride; she read her father's law books; but the highest praise she could win from him was, "Ah, you should have been a boy!" At age twenty-five, against her parents' wishes, Elizabeth married a reform-minded journalist named Henry Stanton. They agreed to omit the word "obey" from their marriage vows. Her family was appalled. The newlyweds' honeymoon was a trip to London for the World Anti-Slavery Convention in 1840. Elizabeth's family didn't like that, either.

Lucretia Coffin Mott (1793-1880) was a Nantucket sea captain's daughter, a devout Quaker, and a schoolteacher who later became a Quaker minister herself. At age eighteen she married a fellow teacher, James Mott, Following Quaker teachings on the evils of slavery, Lucretia gave up using cotton cloth and cane sugar--the products of enslaved people's labor.

Naturally the Motts attended the World Anti-Slavery Convention in London. There, the main floor was for men only. Women had to sit in the balcony and keep quiet. Thus it was that Lucretia Mott and Elizabeth Stanton met at this convention, and they were indignant. Then and there, these two agreed to do something about women's rights. Lucretia was forty-seven; Elizabeth, twenty-five. The two friends vowed to keep in touch. They did, but the demands of marriage and motherhood (Mott had six children, Stanton, seven) kept them apart for eight years.

In the summer of 1848 they finally met, and made a bold decision: they would hold a women's rights convention in the little town of Seneca Falls, New York. The rest, as the saying goes, is history.

Here is their official statement of protest, a feminist

Declaration of Independence. It's long, but well worth reading:

When, in the course of human events, it becomes necessary for one portion of the family of man to assume among the people of the earth a position different from that which they have hitherto occupied, but one to which the laws of nature and of nature's God entitle them, a decent respect to the opinions of mankind requires that they should declare the causes that impel them to such a course.

We hold these truths to be self-evident: that all men and women are created equal; that they are endowed by their Creator with certain inalienable rights; that among these are life, liberty, and the pursuit of happiness; that to secure these rights governments are instituted, deriving their powers from the consent of the governed. Whenever any form of government becomes destructive of these rights, it is the right of those who suffer from it to refuse allegiance to it, and to insist upon the institution of a new government, laying its foundation on such principles, and organizing its powers in such form, as to them shall seem most likely to effect their safety and happiness. . . . .

The history of mankind is a history of repeated injuries and usurpation on the part of man toward woman, having in direct object the establishment of an absolute tyranny over her. To prove this, let facts be submitted to a candid world.

- *He has not ever permitted her to exercise her inalienable right to the elective franchise.*
- *He has compelled her to submit to laws, in the formation of which she had no voice.*
- *He has withheld her from rights which are given to the most ignorant and degraded men—both natives and foreigners.*
- *Having deprived her of this first right as a citizen, the elective franchise, thereby leaving her without representation in the halls of legislation, he has oppressed her on all sides.*
- *He has made her, if married, in the eye of the law, civilly dead.*
- *He has taken from her all right in property, even to the wages she earns.*
- *He has made her morally, an irresponsible being, as she can commit many crimes with impunity, provided they be*

done in the presence of her husband. In the covenant of marriage, she is compelled to promise obedience to her husband, he becoming, to all intents and purposes, her master— the law giving him power to deprive her of her liberty, and to administer chastisement.

- *He has so framed the laws of divorce, as to what shall be the proper causes of divorce, in case of separation, to whom the guardianship of the children shall be given; as to be wholly regardless of the happiness of the women—the law, in all cases, going upon a false supposition of the supremacy of a man, and giving all power into his hands.*

- *After depriving her of all rights as a married woman, if single and the owner of property, he has taxed her to support a government which recognizes her only when her property can be made profitable to it.*

- *He has monopolized nearly all the profitable employments, and from those she is permitted to follow, she receives but a scanty remuneration.*

- *He closes against her all the avenues to wealth and distinction, which he considers most honorable to himself. As a teacher of theology, medicine, or law, she is not known.*

- *He has denied her the facilities for obtaining a thorough education—all colleges being closed against her.*

- *He allows her in church, as well as State, but a subordinate position, claiming Apostolic authority for her exclusion from the ministry, and, with some exceptions, from any public participation in the affairs of the Church.*

- *He has created a false public sentiment by giving to the world a different code of morals for men and women, by which moral delinquencies which exclude women from society, are not only tolerated but deemed of little account in man.*

- *He has usurped the prerogative of Jehovah himself, claiming it as his right to assign for her a sphere of action, when that belongs to her conscience and her God.*

- *He has endeavored, in every way that he could to destroy her confidence in her own powers, to lessen her self-respect, and to make her willing to lead a dependent and abject life.*

Now, in view of this entire disfranchisement of one-half the people of this country, their social and religious degradation—in view of the unjust laws above mentioned, and because women do feel themselves aggrieved, oppressed, and fraudulently deprived of their most sacred rights, we insist that they have immediate admission to all the rights and privileges which belong to them as citizens of these United States.

In entering upon the great work before us, we anticipate no small amount of misconception, misrepresentation, and ridicule; but we shall use every instrumentality within our power to effect our object. We shall employ agents, circulate tracts, petition the State and national Legislatures, and endeavor to enlist the pulpit and the press in our behalf. We hope this Convention will be followed by a series of Conventions, embracing every part of the country.

Sixty-eight women and thirty men signed this document, which for the first time in American history, asked that women be given the right to vote.

Elizabeth Cady Stanton said that "drunkards, idiots, horseracing rumselling rowdies, ignorant foreigners, and silly boys" were able to vote, but women were not. "Have it we must," said Elizabeth, "Use it we will. The pens, the tongues, the fortunes, the indomitable wills of many women are already pledged to secure this right."

One of those women was a black woman who also spoke her mind: Sojourner Truth (1797-1883) stood before an audience of whites in Akron, Ohio in 1851 and gave what became known as the "Ain't I a Woman?" speech.

Here are her words:

Well, children, where there is so much racket there must be something out of kilter. I think that 'twixt the Negroes of the South and the women at the North, all talking about rights, the white men will be in a fix pretty soon. But what's all this here talking about?

That man over there says that women need to be helped into carriages, and lifted over ditches, and to have the best place everywhere. Nobody ever helps me into carriages, or over mud-puddles, or gives me any best place! And ain't I a woman? Look at me! Look at my arm! I have ploughed and planted, and gathered into barns, and no man could head me! And ain't I a woman? I could work as much and eat as much as a man – when I could get it – and bear the lash as well! And ain't I a woman? I have borne thirteen children, and seen most all sold off to slavery, and when I cried out with my mother's grief, none but Jesus heard me! And ain't I a woman?

Then they talk about this thing in the head; what's this they call it? [member of audience whispers, "intellect"] That's it, honey. What's that got to do with women's rights or Negroes' rights? If my cup won't hold but a pint, and yours holds a quart, wouldn't you be mean not to let me have my little half measure full?

Then that little man in black there, he says women can't have as much rights as men, 'cause Christ wasn't a woman! Where did your Christ come from? Where did your Christ come from? From God and a woman! Man had nothing to do with Him.

If the first woman God ever made was strong enough to turn the world upside down all alone, these women together ought to be able to turn it back, and get it right side up again! And now they is asking to do it. The men better let them.

Obliged to you for hearing me, and now old Sojourner ain't got nothing more to say.

Sojourner Truth's eloquence in 1851 stirred audiences, but it did not move them. Women of any color did not get the right to vote until 1920.

African American men got the right to vote, given them by the Fifteenth Amendment, passed by Congress February26, 1869, and ratified February 3, 1870. It says that the right to vote cannot be denied "on account of race, color, or previous condition of servitude."

The 15th Amendment infuriated ardent women's rights advocates. Elizabeth Cady Stanton (who, being a woman, was not allowed access to the U.S. Senate) persuaded Senator Aaron Sargent of California to introduce the following amendment to Congress in 1878:

The rights of citizens of the United States to vote shall not be denied or abridged by the United Sates or any State on account of sex.

Congress shall have the power to enforce this article by appropriate legislation.

This amendment was introduced again and again in every succeeding Congress for the next forty-two years. On August 26,1920. it became part of the Constitution as the Nineteenth Amendment.

Many people opposed it. Here racism comes out of the closet again: denying the vote "on account of sex" meant that all women-- including African American women--would now have the right to vote.

For many Americans, most of them Southerners, giving the vote to African American men had been a hard pill to swallow.

For many Americans, most of them male, giving the right to vote to women, especially African American women, was unthinkable.

This was not a pretty fight. (Neither, for different reasons, is the ongoing battle between Democrats and Republicans over voting in our own time.)

After the long struggle to win the vote, did American women, who had always made up about half the country's population, rush to the polls in the next election and make a difference?

Not exactly.

A woman had already been elected to the House of Representatives: Congress: Jeanette Rankin of Montana was elected in 1916, because Montana allowed women to vote. She was elected to another term in 1940.

In 1932 the first woman elected to the U.S. Senate was Hattie Caraway of Arkansas.

Progress was slow in coming, but it came:

As of 2022, of 100 U.S. Senators, 24 are women.

Of 435 members of the U.S. House of Representatives, 120 are women.

And the Vice President of the United States is a woman.

~

10. Lincoln's Emancipation Proclamation did not end slavery.

Lincoln was known as "the Great Emancipator," but the Emancipation Proclamation of 1863, despite what many people think, did not end slavery. For the back story, we begin with the election of 1860. When the votes were counted, the Republican Abraham Lincoln was the winner. Democrats were in a panic. It was as bad as, maybe even worse, than 2016 when another Republican candidate won and the Democrats awoke the next morning thinking they had had a bad dream. Just like the election of you-know-who, Lincoln as President was a nightmare to half the country. In 1860 there was no arguing over the results (please note): Lincoln got 180 electoral college votes, and the Democrats' darling, Stephen ("The Little Giant") Douglas, got 12. The Democratic Party had serious splits, (Is there a lesson here?) and they had two Democratic candidates running for President. The disaffected Dems ran John Breckenridge, who had been Veep under President James Buchanan (the team was sometimes called "Breck and Old Buck.") Breck got 72 electoral votes. To show you how splintered politics was in those days, there was a fourth horse in this presidential race: John Bell, representing a well-meaning but short-lived group called the Constitutional Union Party. He got 39 electoral votes.

Tensions were so high after Lincoln was declared winner, that Republicans feared for his life. They were terrified of assassination attempts. To transport him from his hometown of Springfield, Illinois, to Washington, D.C. for his inauguration, they draped him in a Scottish plaid shawl and snuck him into the capital on a train separate from that carrying his wife Mary Todd Lincoln.

(Yes, he was assassinated, but not until after the Civil War. John Wilkes Booth shot him at the theater on April 15, 1865, just six days after the war had ended.)

When my class reached this point, in talking about Abraham Lincoln, I had a gimmick. "When the bell rings, and you leave today, if you like, you can stop by the lectern and shake hands with a woman who shook hands with a man who shook hands with Abraham Lincoln." Giggles, nudges, and head-shakings followed. "I'm not that old," I would say. "Let me tell you. When I was about six, my family lived in Fort Stockton, Texas. The old fort's stone buildings were still standing. One day my parents took me to visit an old man who lived in one of them. Judge Oscar Waldo Williams ("Judgie" to his family) was 92. He bent over to shake my hand, and said, "Young lady, I was just about your age when I got to shake hands with Abraham Lincoln. Now you must always remember you shook the hand of a man who shook hands with Abe Lincoln!" So I did. Now, I said to my students, you can shake my hand and pass it on. I trust they have.

More about the Williams family: Judge O.W Williams had a distinguished career, including many years as county judge of Pecos County in the 1880s and 90s. His grandson, Clayton W. Williams, Junior, became briefly more famous when he ran for governor against Ann Richards in 1990—and lost, becoming, so far, the last Texas Republican to lose a race for governor. He lost in 1990 largely because of a crude remark he made long before "Me, Too." If you want to know the details, look him up online.

As I used to tell my students, I knew "Claytie" when he was fourteen and I was eight. My mother taught seventh grade in the Fort Stockton school, and I remember Claytie mostly as a student in her class. When we went on school picnics in Comanche Springs Park, sometimes we would stop and scoop up handfuls of water to quench our thirsts from the Comanche Springs streams that flowed through the park. In the 1940s Comanche Springs bubbled out some sixty million gallons of pure, icy-cold, delicious water every day. Besides the park, it fed farms, too, and best of all, a huge natural swimming-pool, which, thanks to the springs, had a complete change of water about every three minutes. That meant, in the time before we all could get vaccinated to protect us from polio, Comanche Springs pool was safe. In those days, ordinary public swimming pools were considered polio-spreaders.

Polio was a dread disease that crippled and killed thousands. I used to baby-sit for a little girl who had been crippled by polio: one of her legs was shrivelled and floppy, causing her to limp badly. Her mother told me that she would walk lop-sided for the rest of her life. She was just four years old. Polio had killed her older brother. This dread disease could even strike adults. Polio was the reason President Franklin D. Roosevelt wore steel braces on his legs and was wheelchair-bound. I remember how grateful, how relieved we were when a polio vaccine came out in 1955. Everybody rushed to get it, and in a few years the U.S. was polio-free. (Anti-vaxxers, please take note.)

Before we wandered to West Texas, where were we? Now, backward in time, and eastward in space: Why were Democrats, most all of them Southerners, so fired up about Abe Lincoln in 1860? One word will do for an answer: slavery. He was against it. He thought it wrong on moral, political, and economic grounds—but he knew he could not be president of all the nation with those views. As a compromise, he promised he'd not lay a finger on slavery in states where it already existed. There it had to stop: Lincoln was against letting slavery spread into new states. For Southerners that was not enough. They took immediate action. They left the Union.

The election that put Lincoln in the saddle was on November 6, 1860. Six weeks later, on December 20, South Carolina seceded from the Union. (That quaint term, "Union, was what they used to call the United States.) Like ducks in a row, ten other Southern states—Florida, Georgia, North Carolina, Virginia, Alabama, Mississippi, Louisiana, Texas, North Carolina, Tennessee—all followed South Carolina to leave the Union (USA) and form the Confederate States of America (CSA). On April 12, 1861, the first shots were fired by Southern guns on a U.S. fort in Charleston harbor. The Civil War was on.

Faced with a broken Union, President Lincoln had to walk a tightrope if he wanted to save his divided country. On August 22,1862 he wrote a letter to Horace Greeley, founder of the *New York Tribune,* who had been urging him make war against slavery. Said Lincoln: **If I could save the Union without freeing any slave I would do it, and if I could save it by freeing all the slaves I would do it; and if I could save it by freeing some and leaving others alone, I would also do that.**

He chose the last of these options.

The Emancipation Proclamation that Lincoln signed on January 1, 1863. said that *"all persons held as slaves within any State or designated part of a State . . . <u>in rebellion against the United States,</u> shall be then, thenceforward, and forever free."*

Note the underlined words (author's addition). Not ALL states—just those as of January 1863 still in rebellion: that would be all of the Confederate States of America except Tennessee, which was already under Union control. Four other states with enslaved persons—Missouri, Maryland, Delaware, and Kentucky—remained loyal to the Union and did not join the Confederacy, and their enslaved servants were not freed. These states were known as Border States. And with them was West Virginia, which split from its mother state in the middle of the war. Parts of Louisiana and Virginia then under Union control were also exempted.

The Emancipation Proclamation was a war measure: As Union forces moved into the South, a growing number of daring enslaved persons left their masters and ran to the Union soldiers' camps for protection. Then these escapees were "contraband." This was war, and they were enemy property, but what to do with them? President Lincoln's answer was to free them. Under the Emancipation Proclamation they were no longer enslaved. And the able-bodied formerly enslaved men could enlist in the Union army and fight against their former owners. Abolitionists, who had been fighting against slavery since the 1830s, were especially glad about this.

On my father's side I come from a family of abolitionists: In 1839 Daniel and Sarah Purington, my father's grandparents, who lived in Amesbury, Massachusetts, named their daughter Lydia Maria Purington, after Lydia Maria Child, a well-known abolitionist-feminist writer. In 1856 they names a son Charles Sumner, after a famous anti-slavery U.S. Senator). Their eldest son, my great-uncle Dillwyn Varney Purington, born in 1841, enlisted in the Union Army in 1861 at age 20. By December 1863 he was 1st Lieutenant and Quartermaster of the 7th U.S. Colored Troops Regiment, Company S, 7th Infantry. "Colored Troops"— commanded by white officers, of course—would make up about 10 percent of the Union forces, thanks to the Emancipation Proclamation.

The point of this reminiscence is one of my favorite childhood memories, long before I heard of the Civil War. When I was about four years old, my father used to teach me songs to sing with him. One of our favorites was a rousing ditty called "Year of Jubilo." I now know that it was written in 1862, early in the Civil War. I can imagine my father learning it as a child, perhaps from his abolitionist grandparents. He sang the verses, and I joined in on the chorus.

Oh, can you see the master comin' with the mustache on his
face,
Well, he come out here sometime this morning, said he's
gonna leave this place.
He saw the smoke way up the river where the Lincoln
gunboats lay,
And he grabbed his hat and he left mighty sudden, and I
think he's gone away!

CHORUS:
Oh, the master run, ha ha,
And the black folks stay, ho ho!
And it must be now that the kingdom's comin',
In the Year of Jubilo.

Now the overseer, he makes trouble, and he runs us round a
spell,
Well, we locked him up in the smokehouse cellar with the
keys thrown down the well.
His whip is lost, his handcuffs broken and the master'll have
his pay,
He's old enough and big enough and ought to know better
than to went and run away.

In case you didn't get it: This is a song about a Civil War plantation owner who runs away, wearing a fake mustache, fearing capture by the "Lincoln gunboats" in the river. With the master gone, his joyful enslaved servants lock up their overseer and celebrate, singing about the "Year of Jubilo." That was the year of the Emancipation Proclamation.

My father came from abolitionist stock, but my mother came from a family of pro-slavery folks with a plantation in Alabama. Her grandfather (whom she always referred to as "Grandpaw Stanley"), William Henry Stanley, Jr., enlisted in the Confederate army in 1861 as a private in Company C, 5th Alabama Regiment. He was captured during the Battle of the Wilderness in 1864 and spent a freezing winter (no winter clothes, one thin blanket) in a "Yankee" prison in Elmira, New York. After the war William Henry Stanley came to Texas, married, and started a family. The house he built in 1871 stood for 129 years. His many descendants included my grandfather, Ferrin Stanley (the one mentioned earlier) who had six daughters, the eldest being my mother. In 1936, when my Illinois Yankee father came to Texas and wanted to marry my mother, my grandfather happily consented, with one request: "I'll give her to you—if you promise to find husbands for the other five." In the little East Texas town of Tenaha, people shook their heads and said, "Ferrin Stanley's daughter's marrying a Yankee!" Civil War memories last, and last.

I learned just how long those memories last when I taught summer school at my university in the 1970s. One of the students, spending a summer in Houston, was from a little town in Mississippi. After a ninety-minute class on Reconstruction (summer classes had to cover a lot of ground in a short time), this student was waiting for me outside. He was a tall kid, and he towered over me, eyes narrowed in anger, fists clenched.

"I don't like how you talked about the South!"

I stepped back a little, fearing for a tense moment that he was going to hit me. All I could think of to say was "What?"

"Men in my family fought for the Confederacy, and two of 'em died for it! And after the war, people went hungry, and the women had to work like field hands, picking cotton! And black Niggers walked the streets and put on airs!" He stopped for a deep breath. "I wish to God the South had won that war!"

I, too, took a deep breath. Then I said, "I'm sorry, but history is history, and we can't change it, can we? But we can —" He turned and walked away before I could finish that sentence. I knew I couldn't change his mind, no matter what I said. He finished the course, but never spoke to me again. I wonder what became of him.

Back to Lincoln's Emancipation Proclamation: Issued in January 1863, it freed all enslaved people in Confederate states still in rebellion, but enslaved men, women, and children in Texas, at the far western edge of the Confederacy, did not know that, and why would their masters tell them? War news was often sketchy and travelled slowly. In fact, Texas troops fought the last battle of the Civil War—after the war was over. The Battle of Palmito Hill was fought on May 12-13, 1865. In this last battle, near Brownsville, Texas, Confederate forces won. Too late. On April 9, Union forces had defeated Confederates at the Battle of Appomattox Court House (not a court house, but the name of a Virginia village). Then General Robert E. Lee surrendered to General Ulysses S. Grant at Appomattox Court House, actually at the house of one William McLean. (Now you can see all of this if you visit the Appomattox Court House National Historical Park.)

In the spring of 1865 the Civil War was over, but there were still battles to be won.

When the Civil War ended there were over 182,000 enslaved people in Texas, about 30 percent of the whole population. Their masters who read newspapers had known about the Emancipation Proclamation of 1863, but why tell their enslaved servants? Most enslaved people couldn't read, and they need never know. The enslaved men, women, and children on Texas farms and plantations just kept on planting and hoeing, cooking and washing. They did not learn that they were free until two years later, on June 19, 1865. Now we all know that date as the "Juneteenth." In 1865 that was the day that General Gordon Grainger, U.S. Army, assigned to Galveston, read aloud a document making enslaved people in Texas as free as all the rest. You can imagine the joy with which that message was received in some quarters, but white farmers and plantation owners were not thrilled. What happened in Texas during the next ten years, the period known as "Reconstruction" is a fascinating story, with an upside and a downside for African Americans. You can read about it, like the Civil War, in a zillion other books.

Now you know: Slavery in this country officially ended, not with the Emancipation Proclamation on January 1, 1863, but in 1865, when Congress approved the Thirteenth Amendment to the Constitution of the United States, forever ending slavery and "involuntary servitude." On December 6 of that year, 27 of the then

36 states ratified this amendment., and on December 18, 1865 it became the law of the land. Slavery in the United States was now legally dead.

In the years after June 19, 1865 the "Juneteenth" became a day for celebration every summer, and it eventually spread to states outside Texas. It had fireworks and barbecues, picnics and parades, and concerts rivalling the 4th of July, but it was mostly a holiday for African Americans.

In 2021 Congress voted to declare the "Juneteenth" a national holiday.

Progress is often very, very slow.

Speaking of progress, we have now been through the ten true-false questions that began this book, but U.S. history does not end there.

In the old days my U.S. History survey course for the first semester ended with Reconstruction. We all went home for the Christmas break, knowing that the Union was saved. (The word, "Union" has not been used for decades. Nowadays, given the divided state of our politics, it is more than ever a fiction.) The Confederacy and the Old South became the stuff of myth and memory. Years later, some pundit said that the South won the Civil War in novels and movies like *Gone with the Wind*. That film, by the way, is one that every American should see. 1. It's a classic film. 2. It's a perfect example of the racist attitudes in the 1930s and after. When I discovered that more than half my students had never seen it, I told them they were culturally deprived, and showed them the first 30 minutes in class. Then I said if you want to know what happened to Scarlett and the Old South, watch the rest of this on your own. I think most of them did. One year a class had a GWTW watch-party with a supper of ham, fried chicken, biscuits, and field peas.

After the "War Between the States," as some Southern re-enactors still like to call it, the Confederate States of America had folded their flags (Actually, no: The Confederate battle flag, known as the Stars and Bars, became a proud symbol of white supremacy, displayed on automobile bumpers, pickup truck windows, jackets, T-shirts, biceps, baseball caps, and most recently, carried by some members of the mob that stormed the White House in the Battle of January 6, 2021.

The road from Reconstruction to the present is a long and twisted one, but we will just hit some high spots. This part has another true-false quiz:

~

American History: True or False?

1. "Black codes" were laws protecting ex-slaves in the South after slavery ended.

2. The stock market crash of 1929 caused the Great Depression of the 1930s.

3. Roosevelt knew about the attack on Pearl Harbor, but let it happen so the US would join the war.

4. In the Cuban missile crisis, President Kennedy told Soviet Premier Khrushchev that the U.S. would destroy Russia's missile-launch sites in Cuba.

5. After JFK was shot in Dallas, the Warren Commission reported that the assassination was a conspiracy.

6. Woodstock, a monumental outdoor music festival in 1969, turned disastrous when 400,000 people showed up.

7. President Richard M. Nixon was impeached in 1974.

8. The very first computers were hand-held devices, as tiny as transistor radios.

9. Being "gay," (i.e. homosexual) has been socially OK since the "Gay Nineties (i.e., 1890s).

10. Donald J. Trump really had enough votes to win the presidency in 2020.

~

Answers: Are you ready for this:? ALL of the above are FALSE.

If you did not make the grade on this one, keep reading. The right answers may surprise you, and as the old saying goes, the truth may make you free.

As a young professor, for a number of years I taught only the first semester of U.S. history. Senior professors in the history department did the second half. One day at the end of my semester a student came to me and said how much she'd enjoyed being in my class. "Lots of us hope you'll learn the rest of U.S. history so you can teach the second half."

"Thanks," I said, "I'm working on it."

When I did start teaching "U.S. History Since 1877" I ran into a problem my colleagues told me they shared: Students have no sense of time. They look upon all professors as old geezers, having lived through all of the stuff we teach. My years of teaching spanned the 1970s through the early 2000s. We did not realize that we were then living through a time that shook the whole world: the computer and the Internet wrought changes we have yet to master.

When I was in college one of my professors said the world can invent technology to change lives, but society has yet to catch up. I still think about that. We can send a man to the moon, but we can't fix racism. We can put a telescope into space, but we can't conquer a pandemic.

Science and technology are things that I, a history major who squeaked by a required freshman math course and never went to Chemistry 100 lab, do not pretend to understand. I am not alone. One of my favorite teaching memories is from the time I used the D.W. Griffith film, *Birth of a Nation,* in my survey class. (If you've never seen it, do so. You can't make sense of American history without it. President Woodrow Wilson called it "History written with lightning." The National Association of Colored People—NAACP—thought otherwise.)

When I assigned it to my class, I told them to meet me in the viewing room at 6 p.m. "Eat before you come. It's over four hours long."

The next day I walked into class and said, "Let's cut to the chase: what was your first reaction to "Birth of a Nation"?

"You didn't tell us it was silent."

"We didn't know it was in black and white."

Then an excited young woman waved her hand, eager to speak:

"I think it was just wonderful how they got that video of Lincoln's assassination, with Booth jumping down from the balcony onto the stage, and all."

Silence descended in our classroom. Some people turned around to see who had said that.

I put on what I hoped was a tolerant smile. Then I said, "Ah, Miss X (Don't want to embarrass her if she ever reads this book.), let's think for a minute. When was Lincoln assassinated?"

She knew right away: "1865."

"When was TV invented?"

She was not quite sure. "Maybe the 1940s, after World War II?" Then the light suddenly dawned. "Oh!"

I shrugged. Then we both smiled.

That student, like all her contemporaries, had never known a world without television. To them, if it wasn't on TV, it didn't exist.

Another *Birth of a Nation* story: I had never seen the film until I began teaching. When it was shown at a film center near my house, I went. The theater was crowded and already dark when I slipped into a back-row seat. With everybody else, I watched in disbelief at scenes of racial caricatures, with white actors in blackface, alternately leering and grinning, dancing jigs in the street, groping white women, playing newly-freed ex-slaves after the Civil

War. For a 1915 film, what did we expect? Toward the end of the film (spoiler alert!) there is a scene of white-robed, hooded Ku Klux Klan members on horseback, thundering down a road to the climax. At that moment there was a burst of applause from some people in the front row of the theater. There were loud cheers. I knew there were lots of college students in the audience, and I assumed they were making raucous, sarcastic fun of the KKK. I was wrong. At the end of the film the theater lights came on. The front row people stood up all together and marched out. They were wearing black T-shirts with KKK on them. They were for real. Those cheers were for real. The rest of us in the audience rolled our eyes at each other and sat silent, waiting until we thought it was safe to venture out.

Wait, there's more: When I told my class about this adventure, a young man in the front row just a few feet from my lectern looked at me with a grin that gave me goose-bumps. He exited with his classmates as usual, but one of them came back as I was fastening my briefcase and said, "Hey, did you know that X is a member of the KKK?"

For the rest of that term, I was careful not to look him in the eye.

Now for the answers to the new quiz. Unlike the first ten questions, all ten of these are FALSE.

~

1. "Black codes" were laws protecting ex-slaves in the South after slavery ended.

Slavery ended in 1865 with the Thirteenth Amendment to the Constitution, but what were some four million ex-slaves going to do then? Now there would be a dozen or so government agencies created to ease their pathway to freedom. Back then, there was only one: the Freedmen's Bureau, whose full title was "Bureau of Refugees, Freedmen, and Abandoned Lands." Pitifully understaffed and under-funded, it was supposed to look after the needs of whites as well as all freed people after the dislocations of war. That meant medical, educational, legal—all kinds of needs. Thousands of freed people wanted to search for family members who'd been sold away from them. In the meantime, Southern states took the bit between their collective teeth and began passing laws to control what they considered to be "uppity" freedmen and women. Mississippi (for many years a front-runner in racism) led off in 1865 with a law that all Black people must have a written contract each January for their labor the coming year, and if they quit before that year was out, they'd lose all their wages and might go to jail. How's that for slavery by another name? But wait, there's lots more: In Tennessee a handful of white guys formed a secret club they called the "Ku Klux Klan." They took that name from the Greek "kuklos" meaning cycle or circle, and the English word "clan" meaning society or tribe. Little did they dream how famous—or infamous—that name would become. They designed costumes of white robes and hoods, and went around scaring Blacks who first thought they were ghosts. Then the KKK got lots more members, and got lots more inventive. We won't go there.

In 1865 South Carolina, not to be outdone in Black Codes, passed a law that forbade Blacks to be anything farmers or servants. If you were Black and wanted to be a blacksmith or a barber or follow any other calling, you had to pay a tax of up to $100 every year. In the Confederate states just after the Civil War, very few people—black or white—had that kind of cash. Other states quickly fell into line with their own black codes. In much of what had been the Old South, Black people could be arrested for "vagrancy," i.e., being on the streets, looking for work, preaching without a license, renting or buying property, "disturbance of the peace," or almost anything a white person wanted to invent. Blacks were not to serve on juries unless for an all-black trial. Voting? We won't go there.

What was going on in our nation's capital? Abe Lincoln was dead, and the new President Andrew Johnson was not one of our best. He would be impeached (tried, but not convicted) in 1868.

Congress finally managed to get its act together, and added some useful amendments to the Constitution:

The Fourteenth Amendment of 1868 promised that no state could "deprive any person of life. Liberty, or property, without due process of law."

The Fifteenth Amendment of 1870 promised that "the right of citizens of the United States to vote shall not be denied or abridged by the United States or by any State on account of race, color, or previous condition of servitude." Slavery, yes, is out. But race and color? Think about it. Then think some more.

Besides *Gone With the Wind* and *Birth of a Nation*, there were other films we used in class. I sometimes began the first day of "U.S. Since 1877" with a scene from Spike Lee's 1989 *Do the Right Thing*. We would watch an altercation between Sal, an Italian deli owner and Radio Raheem, an African American known for his "boom box." The scene happens one night in a Brooklyn neighborhood after Sal breaks Raheem's radio with a baseball bat. Police arrive. There is a struggle, and, in a scene all too familiar decades later, a policeman chokes Radio Raheem to death. At that moment, I would turn off the film and say to my class, "What did you see happen here?" The answers were always varied.

"A black guy picked a fight with a white guy and got killed."

"A white policeman choked a black guy."

"It was too dark to see what really happened."

That's what history is all about, I used to say. People don't see things the same way. Different backgrounds, different points of view, different reasons for telling a story one way or another. Historians try to figure out what's true and not true. Remember that.

On the first day of class I used to ask a riddle:

What do John the Baptist, Peter the Great, and Kermit the Frog have in common?

This met with puzzled stares. Nobody ever got it.

Then I would grin and say,

"Same middle name!"

Historians, I would say, have to look for connections in unexpected places. That's part of their job.

~

2. The stock market crash of 1929 caused the Great Depression of the 1930s.

Later on in my U.S. Since 1877 class we also watched the first half hour of John Ford's *Grapes of Wrath*. What better way to introduce the devastation of the Great Depression of 1930s? We saw a bleak landscape ravaged by the Dust Bowl (One of my students kept calling it the "Dusty Bowl," which is as good a way as any to remember it). As *Grapes of Wrath* began, we watched farmers' frame houses bulldozed to the ground by orders of government people they'd never seen. We watched as the Joad family were forced off their family's land, and we saw them pack up their meager belongings. I warned my class that one scene always makes me cry, and I don't remember crying in a movie since I was seven and saw *Lassie Come Home.* When Jane Darwell, as the matriarch of the Joad family, holds a pair of dangly earrings up to her weather-beaten ears and looks in a mirror, remembering happier times, I tear up. I can't help it.

Grapes of Wrath is a good jumping-off place for learning about the Depression. We still capitalize it, even today. I used to say to my classes, We call it the Great Depression because we've never had another one so great—at least, not so far. On the other hand, people called World War I "the Great War"—until World War II outdid it in greatness. Some day another history class may look back at us and say, Why didn't they see X coming? (For X substitute pandemics, climate change, war, etc.) In the Great Depression many people in the 1930s lost their jobs, lost their savings, went hungry. How come? My students would ask. They were too young to know.

Many people thought the "Roaring Twenties" caused the Depressed Thirties: The nation went on a decade-long party, spending money and dancing the Charleston, and buying stocks with wild abandon, and one Tuesday, October 29, in 1929 the stock market crashed, and a lot of people lost a lot of money, and that caused the Great Depression. Not so. Historians like to tell you there are many causes for nearly everything, and that is true here. If you want a running start for the Depression, go back to World War I, when Europe lost a generation of young men, not to mention many farms and factories. Germany got stuck with a huge war debt to make it pay for its role in the war. Cash was scarce in Europe, so who did Germany borrow money from to pay back its war debts ? The richest nation in the world: the United States of America. Wall Street and banks made loans to Germany, to the rest of Europe, and one thing led to another. As an economics professor friend of mine once told me, the Great Depression happened mainly because people were spending money they didn't have. Lots of things came together, I would tell my students. The rest of what I said is too long to put into this book. The billions of dollars lost when stocks tumbled in 1929 was one of many things that triggered a decade of a depressed national economy—but it was not THE cause.

A friend of mine whose father worked for one of the big Wall Street firms in 1929 told me a Depression story. Her father said that on Black Tuesday over 16 million shares of stock were traded in that one day, and the stock tickers couldn't keep up with the transactions. "We were knee deep in ticker tape," he said. "I didn't go home for days."

The Depression soon came to Texas. My grandfather Ferrin Stanley (remember him?) owned a grocery store in Tenaha, Texas, a place with a population of about six or seven hundred people. "Mr. Ferrin" was known and loved by everybody. He used to dress up as Santa at Christmas and give out candy to children. When his wife presented him with twin daughters to go with the four daughters they already had, he put up a sign over his store that read, "J.F. Stanley and Daughters." An inside joke. But the Depression was no joke. Many people couldn't pay their grocery bills. Ferrin Stanley knew them all, and he gave them groceries on credit until at last he himself went bankrupt and had to close his store. Eventually he and his family moved to Austin, Texas, where they ran a very successful boarding house at 1511 Colorado, just up the hill behind the state capitol. That white stone mansion, built before the Civil War, is now the headquarters of the Texas Historical Commission. The old stone picnic table in the back garden, where Ferrin Stanley's twin daughters and their teenage friends once carved their initials in the soft limestone, is still there.

~

3. Roosevelt knew about the attack on Pearl Harbor, but let it happen so the US would join the war.

After the Great Depression came World War II. One day a group of 4th-graders visited my class as we were finishing a discussion of the war. At the end, I said, would our visitors like to ask any questions? A little boy's hand shot up. "Were you alive in World War II?" Titters from my students.

"Yes," I said, "but I was a lot younger than you."

Americans love conspiracy theories, and one that still has legs is that President Franklin Roosevelt knew in advance that Japan was going to attack the U.S. naval base at Pearl Harbor. Not true. I got some unexpected evidence of that from a student: she raised her hand when we were discussing the conspiracy theory and said, My great-uncle was a commander or an admiral—I forget which—but it doesn't matter—he was in a meeting of the U.S Navy high command at the Pentagon on December 7, and they were discussing how to respond to a Japanese attack. U. S. intelligence had told them one was coming, but not where or when. Then an aide came in and said "the Japanese have just attacked Pearl Harbor." Nearly 2500 American lives were lost that day, in the worst attack on this country until 9/11. Before Pearl Harbor many Americans were not for joining a war that had been on since 1939, but after Pearl Harbor nearly everybody jumped aboard the war wagon.

On Pearl Harbor day I was barely four years old. On Sunday afternoons my father and I always went upstairs and took a nap while my mother did the Sunday-roast-beef dinner dishes. On that Sunday she suddenly raced up the stairs. I heard her shout to my dozing father, "Get up! The Japanese have bombed Pearl Harbor!" as though she expected him to leap up and make everything all right. My four-year-old self almost believed that he could do that. What my father did do the next day was to record President Franklin D. Roosevelt's famous "day that will live in infamy" speech. We had a newfangled machine with a turntable and phonograph that could actually cut plastic records of radio programs in real time or cut records of family sing-alongs. (We used to have a record of four-year-old me singing "Year of Jubilo" and "You Are My Sunshine." Fortunately it crumbled away with age.) I remember my father on the phone from his office the morning of December 8, calling home, telling my mother step by step how to make a record of what FDR was about to say. That is why I grew up with a vivid memory of December 7, 1941.

As that war went on, it touched my life in other small ways. I was a talkative child, and also an only child. My doting parents usually let me chatter away, but suddenly not when the radio news was on. "HUSH!" they would say to me as they crouched over our living-room radio to hear the latest war news. (Must I remind you that there was no TV in living rooms in the 1940s?) Then there were the air raid drills. In Fort Worth, Texas, as in other cities, we had to turn off lights and practice black-outs. I was afraid of the dark, anyway, and to sleep without a nightlight in my room really scared me. I also developed a fear that Jap (that's what we called them then) planes would fly over and bomb us like they had Pearl Harbor. For a long time I refused to play by myself outside, and when I did go out again, I kept an eye on the skies.

My father wanted to fight, and tried to enlist in the army, but he was a family man, 41 years old. Instead, as a civil engineer, he worked long hours six days a week for a company that built aircraft plants. We were spared the sorrow of losing someone we loved in the war, but I soon learned that such things happened. One day when I was visiting my grandparents in Austin, one of my teen-aged twin aunts was in her room crying. When I asked why, the other twin said "Scotty's dead. Killed in action on Okinawa." I didn't know what "in action" meant, and I'd never heard of Okinawa, but I knew Scotty as my aunt's funny boyfriend, who sometimes bounced me on his knee and told jokes. Scotty was the only person I ever knew who died in World War II. He was nineteen.

I did have a cousin who fought through the whole war in the Pacific. When it was over, he came to visit us in his uniform as a U.S. Army sergeant. He brought me a pendant he had made for me from an Australian coin. It was a silvery heart with my initials, VNP, on it. I treasure it to this very day. While he was staying with us, my parents left us on Halloween to go to a party, and while they were gone some Halloween tricksters threw something against our front door. My cousin leaped up as if he had been shot, and flung open the door. The offenders had already fled, and he turned to me and apologized.

"That's battle fatigue," my father told me afterward. "Or some call it shell-shock."

Fast forward to the years when I taught World War II: Sometimes I asked my students to do an oral history project, to find someone (besides me) who remembered World War II and interview them. I wish I had made copies of some of those papers. All I remember now is fragments: One student went to a senior living facility, where she talked with a woman who spoke "with an accent." My student noticed a purple number tattooed on the woman's arm, and came to ask my advice:

"I think that was a Holocaust death camp tattoo," she said. "Should I ask her?"

I said ask her if she wants to talk about it. The next day that student came to my office again and said, "She looked at me, and her eyes were so sad. Then she shook her head and said, 'No.'"

Another student sought out an elderly priest, a member of our university faculty. What she learned dumbfounded us all. This mild-mannered, gray-haired priest said, "I was a gunner in the Canadian Air Force." Then, with a laugh, he added, "I was a young guy back then, and I thought being an air force gunner would impress the girls." That story soon went viral, as we would say today, much to the ex-gunner's amusement.

Other war history memories were not so amusing: a young girl from the Philippines interviewed her mother, and found out that her mother's grandparents were resistance fighters when the Japanese took over the Philippines in World War II: "They were wealthy landowners who pretended to cooperate. My grandmother would have dinner parties for the Japanese high command, to keep them distracted while my grandfather organized resistance fighters in the fields behind the house."

For many years I taught a course called World War II in Films. In the 1980s, some of you may recall, Blockbuster stores rented movies on VHS tapes. For the first time, you could watch a film on your living room TV screen. Soon some history majors raised money to buy a TV and a player for the department, and said, we want you to do a course about World War II movies. I said, I'm a colonialist who happens to teach the U.S. survey. I don't pretend to know a bean about World War II. If I do a course about it you'll have to do all the work. Little did I dream they'd say yes, and that the result was one of the best teaching memories I have to this day. We chose ten World War II movies, only those made between 1939 and 1945. No modern stuff. We assigned each film to a team to do research on the background history and the reviews of the film. This was pre-IMDB, and that meant hours in the library looking in real books and magazines (If you want a trip back in time, try old *Life* magazines). Then somebody said, "We have a historical background committee, and a film history committee, but we need a food committee, too." This was to be an evening class once a week, from 5:30 to 8:15 pm.

Nineteen students signed up. We met in the living room of the History House. People came early to stake claims to couch and chairs; latecomers sat on the floor. One said, "It's just like hunkering down with your family to watch TV." We had popcorn. We had chips and dips. We had cookies and M&M's, washed down with canned sodas. We all gained several pounds that semester.

We watched films that were made in Hollywood from 1939 to 1945. Here's a list:

Why We Fight
Buck Privates
The Great Dictator
Air Force
Wake Island
Thirty Seconds Over Tokyo
Bataan
Back to Bataan
North Star
Since You Went Away

If you want to know more, you can look them up online. You can probably see them, too. In the old days I had to go to an audio/video store that carried old films and rent them as videotapes.

One of our aims was to analyze these films for propaganda. All movies made during the war had to meet the requirements set by the Office of War Information. Basically, a Hollywood film had to answer the question, "Will this movie help win the war?"

By the end or our war films class, students had their own list of must-haves:

No blood showing on US military who get killed.

Mothers have gray hair, wear aprons, and bake apple pies.

Every movie needs to have soldiers and sailors from all over the US: one Southerner, one from Brooklyn, one from a farm in the Midwest, etc. No Black guys.

Soldier who shows girlfriend's picture at the beginning is a goner.

Cigarettes never run out, even when ammunition does.

This was one of the best classes ever. I repeated it every other year, with some variations. Later I broadened it to "War in Films." Students all agreed that *All Quiet on the Western Front* was the best war film of all time, and that every diplomat should see it regularly. We included films like the 1968 *Green Berets*, with John Wayne. In that one, when the sun sets in a glorious golden sunset at the end, students rolled on the floor and howled with laughter. "They're in Vietnam, and they're watching a sun setting in the east!"

I never grew tired of teaching that class, but how many times, I thought, can I sit through *Apocalypse Now* and *Saving Private Ryan*?

In this "hitting the high spots" of 20th-century U.S. history, after World War II there was the Cold War. Why that name? Because it was not, and nobody wanted it to be, a Hot War, i.e., a shooting, bombing war. Especially a bombing war, since the A-Bomb (what we called the atomic bomb in those days after we used it on Japan at the end of World War II). Soon there was an even more powerful H- (for hydrogen) Bomb. The Cold War was on, because two superpowers were sworn enemies: the United States (U.S.) and Russia (U.S.S.R., Union of Soviet Socialist Republics) were now facing off. One was a democratic republic; one was a Communist regime. Soon each of them reportedly had enough nuclear power to blow up the world. (Does history repeat itself, or what?)

The brief Korean War (1950-1953) was the first "hot war" of the Cold War, when North Korea (backed by Russia and China, Communists) invaded South Korea (backed by United Nations and U.S. forces, anti-Communists). It ended in a draw, so to speak, with North Korea and South Korea bitter enemies. None of my students chose to interview anybody about this war, but one day when I was lecturing about it, a young man in my class raised his hand and said, "I'm from South Korea, and North Korea is a threat to the world to this very day! People don't realize how much—" His face was flushed, and he was choking on his anger. "Now we know," I told him. "Thanks." That was in the 1990s. Little did we know then how right he was.

The decade after World War II was when fears of a nuclear war kept people awake at night, and teachers taught school children to "duck and cover" under their desks in case of a nuclear attack. Given the horrific force of such an attack, what possible good would that do them? Maybe practicing that move made them or the grown-ups feel better. Fears of a nuclear blow-up were real, because Americans were afraid that Communists were out to destroy us.

I shared a personal memory of Communist fears with my classes:

In the late 1940s we were living in Bartlesville, Oklahoma, then a town of about 25,000, best known for being the home of Phillips Petroleum, whose founder, Frank Phillips, lived in a 26-room mansion in the middle of town. I remember him because he gave Bartlesville school children a Christmas variety show on the stage of a local movie house, with every kid getting a quarter (a lot of money in those days) and a bag of candy. I was a Girl Scout then, and we knew we could count on the Phillips mansion for cookie sales. "Always go to the back door, the service entrance." No matter how many Girl Scouts with cookies showed up, they always made a sale. Frank Phillips died in 1950 at age 77. R.I.P.

In the late 40s in Bartlesville, as everywhere, fears of Communism were spreading faster than you could eat a box of Girl Scout Thin Mints. The librarian of the Bartlesville Public Library, as I recall her, a middle-aged lady with gold-rimmed glasses whose life was her library, was suspected of secretly circulating "Communist literature." She lived for her job, which she thought included monitoring what school kids read in the summer: For every Nancy Drew or Hardy Boys mystery you checked out, you had to check out one other book. She was not a woman to be messed with. One day my father, who was then the city manager of Bartlesville, got a phone call from the FBI. They had reason to suspect the city's librarian was a Communist, because they had heard rumors of Communist books and pamphlets in the library. My father said that was news to him, and he thought it was nonsense. So did the librarian (we'll call her Miss X) Other people in Bartlesville got wind of this, and took sides.

Either you believed that Communism was creeping into our town, or you believed Miss X and my father, and a bunch of other people. We were tarred with a Communist brush. We got threatening phone calls. So did Miss X. People drove past our house in the wee hours and shined bright lights in our windows. This made my mother nervous, and when my father had to be out of town overnight, she armed herself with my little brother's Ray Gun (a '40s toy with a blinding bright light and a loud buzz). "If they come by, I'll aim this at them," she said. Then the FBI agents came to Bartlesville. They, along with my father, conducted a search of the library, with flashlights in the dark of night. (The FBI works in mysterious ways.) They found not one scrap, not one leaflet, not one book, of "Communist literature." That was the Cold War in Bartlesville, Oklahoma. It was much worse in other places.

The Cold War destroyed careers. It produced Senator Joseph McCarthy, who made national news by spreading stories that the U.S. government was riddled with Communists. From 1950 to 1954 he kept a nation on edge with rumors. (Fake news, as we all know, can be dangerous stuff.) If you want the details, look on Google. And you can always watch those end-of-the-world movies. My all-time favorite is "Dr. Strangelove." That was made in the 1968, and it still makes me laugh—and shudder.

I used to ask my American history classes, "Did "The Sixties" really begin in 1960? The collective answer was always, "No." Keep reading, and you'll see why.

In the 1960s there was lots of talk about the "Generation Gap," way before the Digital Age began. That "Gap" was between young people with long hair and tie-dyed T-shirts and mini-skirts and their stodgy parents; between Bo Diddley and Guy Lombardo, between marijuana and Marlboros. Bob Dylan's song, "The Times They Are a-Changin'" caught something in the air. He was working on it before John F. Kennedy's assassination on November 22, 1963, and Dylan opened a concert with it the very next night. This is not a memoir about politics, but JFK's passing was a kind of turning point. After that, the time we call "The Sixties" began. Just before that, there was the Cuban Missile Crisis.

~

4. In the Cuban missile crisis, President Kennedy told Soviet Premier Khrushchev that the U.S. would destroy Russia's missile-launch sites in Cuba.

In October 1962 U.S. aerial photos revealed that there were Russian missile bases in Cuba. These were for missiles that could hit the United States, only 90 miles away. One missile was already in place. That was when the U.S. and Russia came within a hair's-breadth, or maybe just a missile shot, of nuclear war. President Kennedy ordered a blockade around Cuba to keep more missile shipments from landing. If the Russian ships did not turn back, Russia would be sorry. Historians as usual have not yet settled on how we should view this crisis, but for nearly two weeks ("Thirteen Days" as Robert F. Kennedy called it in his memoir) Americans lived from Nightly News to Nightly News (We still had only three major networks in those days, and we trusted all of them to give it to us straight.) Was the world we'd only seen in scary movies like *On the Beach* about to be real? Were we on the edge of nuclear war?

In October 1962 my husband Jim and I were in Houston, and our daughter Catherine was about four months old. We lived in a tiny apartment that had a big closet, the kind built under a flight of stairs.

What will we do if there's a nuclear attack? I said to Jim.

What we did, as I used to tell my classes, was to put a case of Gerber's baby food (Catherine did not yet drink beer) and a case of Lone Star beer (food value: hops are nutritious, we told each other) We can hunker in that closet and hope for the best. We didn't have to. At last, the Russians blinked first. The Russian ships headed for Cuba turned back. The U.S. blockade worked, and Premier Nikita Khrushchev and President John F. Kennedy agreed to settle things more or less peaceably. Russia agreed to no missiles in Cuba, and the U.S. promised not to attack Cuba. (We had already tried that earlier in a failed Bay of Pigs invasion in 1961, but that's another story.) In a secret deal not revealed for twenty-five years, the U.S. also agreed to remove its own missiles from Turkey, which could hit Russia. That gave Khrushchev a way to save face, and it was the off-ramp from escalation to nuclear war. That was then, and we hope it stays then.

~

5. After JFK was shot in Dallas, the Warren Commission reported that the assassination was a conspiracy.

And now we come to 1963, and one (alas, not the only) "where were you when—" moment in recent decades. On November 22, 1963, President John F. Kennedy was assassinated in Dallas, Texas. I was in Allentown, Pennsylvania, where Jim was teaching English fifteen hours a week to freshmen at Muhlenberg College. I was then a stay-at-home mom with Catherine, age eighteen months, and Paul, an infant nearly four months old. On that fateful morning Jim called me from his office on campus and said, "Turn on the TV. We've just heard that Kennedy's been shot in Dallas."

While the Muhlenberg campus turned into chaos, Jim came home (we lived a block from the college). Leaving our toddler and our infant to fend for themselves, the two of us sat down cross-legged on the floor in front of the TV, looking up at it, as if we were imploring that hulking black box with its black-and-white images to tell us that JFK was OK. Yes, there were easy chairs in our living room, and we could have sat in them, but we were in shock. Maybe he's just wounded, we told each other. Then Walter Cronkite took slowly took off his horn-rimmed glasses, laid them on his desk, and said the awful words that told us the worst.

That was Friday, November 22, 1963. From that moment until Monday, November 25, when John Fitzgerald Kennedy was buried in Arlington National Cemetery, the hours and days of that nightmare weekend blurred. All I remember is watching TV non-stop, poking pablum at my son in his infant seat on the breakfast table, sometimes missing his mouth. We went mechanically through the motions of daily life as the TV stayed on. From Friday afternoon through the Monday funeral, there was live coverage: nothing else on ABC, CBS, and NBC, the nation's three major networks. All other programming that weekend was suspended. (This, my students always found hard to believe.)

We watch it all: the landing of Air Force One in Washington in the gray-blue evening light, Jacqueline Kennedy still in her pink blood-spattered suit, the now-President Lyndon B. Johnson looking stone-faced and grim, the startling on-screen assassination of the suspected assassin, Lee Harvey Oswald; the crowds lined up for JFK's lying-in-state in the Capitol rotunda; little John Kennedy, Jr.'s salute to his father's flag-draped casket; the solemn procession with the black horse and the empty saddle, Jacqueline Kennedy regal and sad in her black veil. You know all of this, even if you are too young to have been there. It is the stuff of countless books and several movies. JFK's assassination was made more dramatic by instant conspiracy theories. To quell them, President Johnson ordered the President's Commission on the Assassination of President Kennedy, or Warren Commission for short, because it was led by the respected Supreme Court Chief Justice Earl Warren. After a year of investigation the Warren report found that only one man, Lee Harvey Oswald, was guilty of killing JFK. (Yes, even then, people wanted to blame something or someone for things that seemed inexplicable. If you thought conspiracy theories were new in American history, how many have you seen so far in this book?)

A nation mourned, but life went on. At Muhlenberg college, English majors had a long-planned bus trip to New York to see Edward Albee's hit play, *Who's Afraid of Virginia Woolf?* We went. *Virginia Woolf* is not exactly a feel-good play, and none of us was feeling good to start with.

On the way home late that night in the darkened bus, nobody was talking. Then, from the back of the bus, a sweet soprano voice began began to sing softly, "Where Have All the Flowers Gone?" One by one, other voices joined in. Soon everybody on that bus was singing. When we reached the last verse,

Where have all the graveyards gone?
Gone to flowers, every one
When will they ever learn?
When will they ever learn?

everyone on that bus was weeping. We were weeping for JFK, for our country, for ourselves. Then somebody started the song all over again. We sang that song, tears running down our faces, all the way home.

One other personal note on JFK's assassination (We have to call it that, to distinguish it from—spoiler alert—another Kennedy assassination): In the late 60s my husband was an arts manager in Houston, and several nationally and internationally famous concert artists and dance companies declined bookings in Texas, because of JFK's assassination in Dallas.

John Fitzgerald Kennedy was not the only public figure to die by an assassin's bullet in the '60s. Malcolm X, a powerful black voice for civil rights, was shot in a Manhattan ballroom on February 21,1965. Martin Luther King, Jr., leading the civil rights struggle, was shot on a motel balcony in Memphis, April 4, 1968. While a nation grieved and rioted in rage after that death, Robert Kennedy, JFK's younger brother, running for President in '68, was shot in a Los Angeles hotel on June 5. Their funerals were all on TV.

When General (and former President) Dwight Eisenhower died of natural causes in 1969 and had a state funeral on TV, our six-year-old son Paul happened to pass through the room while I was watching.

"What's that?' he said.

"General Eisenhower's funeral," I said

Without missing a step, Paul kept on walking. "Who shot him?"

The 1960s were the first time we all got used to violent, unexpected events on our TV screens. Here we pass over the burnings and beatings of the Freedom Riders in 1961, the Birmingham church bombings that killed four little Black girls in 1963, the murder of three civil rights workers—two white, one Black— in Mississippi in 1964, the "Bloody Sunday," March 7, 1965, when a march for voting rights turned into a beating of the marchers and a 25-year-old John Lewis got a fractured skull, and the deaths by violence of many others in the struggle for civil rights.

In 1964 the Civil Rights Act outlawed discrimination based on race, color, religion, and sex.

Nearly sixty years, nearly two generations later, we're not there yet. How come?

In 1965 the Voting Rights Act outlawed literacy tests, poll taxes, and other discriminatory practices designed to discourage African Americans from voting.

We're still not quite there. Literary tests and poll taxes are gone, but many states and counties have invented new ways to keep minorities from voting.

On poll taxes: When I, a native Texan, went away to graduate school in Pennsylvania in 1960, my classmates at Penn looked on me as a curiosity. They were amused by my Southern drawl. (I was polite enough not to point out their various Yankee accents.) They were even more fascinated when I mentioned something about paying my poll tax. (This was an election year, and I was voting absentee.)

"Really?" they said, "What does a poll tax look like? Can we see it?"

Poll taxes are now as extinct as dinosaurs, but how come we are still trying to protect voting rights for so many?

The above two questions are more difficult and more important than any of the ten true-false ones that began this book.

I don't have any answers.

Now, switching to a lighter mode before we leave that puzzling decade called The Sixties: I once taught a course with that name. Like my World War II film class, it met once a week in the evenings. One of those evenings was for music. If you really want to understand how American culture changed in the Sixties, I told my students, you have to hear the music. Next week we are going to have a non-verbal class. (I remembered a non-verbal party in the Sixties when I was in graduate school. My husband and I circulated and smiled and danced with our peers in a house fragrant with the smell of marijuana. Did we ever smoke weed? Not at that party, but we had a babysitter who offered to bring us some Acapulco Gold. We said no thanks. We are the parents of three young children, Jim said, we have to be responsible. We did try smoking pot once, but that's another story.) I told my Sixties class, we'll play pop hits from the late Fifties to the early Seventies, non-stop. We won't talk. We're just going to listen. If you want to dress like the Sixties and dance, feel free.

When I told a colleague of mine who used music in lots of his classes what I wanted to do, he sent me two cassette tapes (who remembers those?) with these songs. If he ever reads this book, he'll know who I mean.

If you want to know what we played, here's the list:

Kingston Trio: "Scotch and Soda," "Worried Man," "Greenback Dollar" (1950s)

Weavers: "This Land is Your Land" *(1958)*, "Last Night I Had the Strangest Dream" (1963)

Isley Brothers: "Twist & Shout" (1962)

Paul & Paula: "Hey Paula" (1963)

Joan Baez: "Medgar Evers Lullaby" (1964)

Bob Dylan: "Blowin' in the Wind," "The Times They Are A'changin'" (1963), "Rainy Day   Women" (1966)

Dion: "Abraham, Martin, and John" (1968)

Beach Boys: "Surfin' USA," "Surfer Girl," "California Girls" (1963)

Beatles: "Twist and Shout" (1963), "I Want to Hold Your Hand," "I Saw Her Standing There," "Please Please Me" (1964), "Sgt. Pepper's Lonely Hearts Club Band," "She's Leaving Home" (1967), "Revolution" *(*1968)

Animals: "House of the Rising Sun," "Story of Bo Diddley" (1964)

Rolling Stones: "Time is On My Side," "Satisfaction" (1965), "Street Fighting Man' (1968)

Barry McGuire: "Eve of Destruction" (1965)

The Who: "My Generation" (1965)

The Small Faces: "Itchycoo Park" (1967)

The Doors: "Light My Fire" (1967)

Jefferson Airplane: "White Rabbit" (1967)

Cast of *Hair*: "Aquarius" "Initials," "Don't Put It Down," "Black Boys," "White Boys" (1968), "My Conviction" (1968)

Graham Nash: "Chicago" (1971)

Marvin Gaye: "I Heard It Through the Grapevine" (1968)

Jimi Hendrix: "Star Spangled Banner" (1969)

Crosby, Stills, & Nash: "Ohio" (1970)

John Prine: "Your Flag Decal Won't Get You Into Heaven Any More," "Sam Stone" (1971)

Don McLean: "American Pie" (1971)

At the end of that class, when we talked, all agreed that we could feel the change from cheerful harmony to bitter discord.

In the Sixties a book club I'd been in since college days descended from ladylike literary discussions and elaborate desserts with whipped cream, to shouting political arguments while sitting on the floor and passing around a bottle of bourbon. (We got past that time and are now back to literary ruminations.)

Much, but not all, of the discord of the Sixties was because of the Vietnam War. U.S. involvement began in 1954, to help South Vietnam (democratic) fight invading North Vietnam (Communist). Politicians and professors back then talked learnedly and ominously about a "domino theory," meaning that if South Vietnam fell to the Communists, the other nations in Southeast Asia would soon go down to the Communists like a row of dominos, one after the other. U.S. involvement "escalated," as our government liked to say in those days, in the early Sixties. and in 1964 President Lyndon Johnson sent the first ground troops to Vietnam. U.S. forces did not leave there until 1975.

To put it mildly, many Americans at home were not happy about this war. As for me, I went from a bumper sticker that said "War is not Healthy for Children and Other Living Things" to an anti-war discussion/protest group of 75 or 80 friends in our living room. We called ourselves "Citizens for Disengagement in Vietnam." We all agreed on no street protests, and as one of us put it, "We'll wear socks with our sandals." We soon outgrew the Bernhard living room. We met in a larger venue once a month, promoted anti-war books, and invited like-minded speakers. Once we had a Vietnamese monk who read his poems. But the war went on. And on.

The year 1968 was a bad year in many ways, in the war, when many Americans believed that their government had not been telling the truth (does that sound famliar?), in the assassinations mentioned earlier, and in the presidential election of 1968 when politics, the war, and racism all got mixed together. President Lyndon Johnson, perhaps tired of anti-war crowds chanting "Hey, hey, LBJ! How many kids did you kill today?" decided not to run again. Robert Kennedy was dead. Vice-president Hubert Humphrey took up the Democratic Party banner, and Richard Nixon was his Republican opponent. And there was George Wallace, an Arkansas governor famous for saying,"Segregation now, segregation tomorrow, segregation forever," muddying the waters as an Independent. Tensions, racial, pro-war, and anti-war, ran high.

For example, in Houston there was an annual Press Club Gridiron show, making good-natured satirical fun of public figures and issues. My husband was the director of that show for several years. In 1968 one of the skits was about George Wallace, and the joke was, a Black man in whiteface was set to play him. That man was a respected journalist, a good friend of ours. When news of this skit leaked, the Press Club began getting threats about having a Black man portray Governor Wallace. There were calls saying "If he goes on, he's gonna get shot."

My husband, as director of the show, told the Black journalist he was free to drop out. There was definitely danger involved if he went onstage as Wallace in whiteface.

"No way!" was the answer. "That's just what they want—to scare me! I'm staying in!"

Showtime, on a stage in a huge hotel ballroom with an audience of seven or eight hundred, was very nervous-making. Security was tight. There were police outside. There were police inside.Who knew what might happen?

By some miracle, the Wallace skit went off perfectly, and the star, perspiring more than usual in his whiteface makeup, took a bow to a storm of applause.

That summer of 1968 we watched TV, once again in disbelief, as the Democratic Party convention in Chicago switched to scenes of violence in the streets outside. The scene had been set earlier, when anti-war groups vowed to make their voices heard at the convention. Students for a Democratic Society (SDS) and Youth International Party (Yippies) aimed to show up. The mayor of Chicago, Richard Daley, denied them protest permits. Yippies (Hippies with a political agenda and an in-your-face sense of humor) vowed to come to Chicago anyway and wreak havoc. They threatened to put LSD (lysergic acid diethylglamide, a halllucenogenic substance famous in the 60s) in the convention hall's water supply and bring sexy young women to seduce stoned male delegates. They nominated their own candidate for president, a pig named "Pigasus."

Chicago's Mayor Daley put barbed-wire barricades around the convention center and placed 11,000 policemen and 6,000 Illinois National Guardsmen on alert. To make a long story short, when 10,000 protesters arrived in Chicago, hell broke loose. Policemen began beating and clubbing youthful protesters, injuring many, as the now-uneasy proceedings lurched forward inside the convention center.

A friend of mine told me how she remembered that night. Her parents lived in Chicago, and her father was a retired Episcopal priest.

That awful evening he got a phone call from a colleague. "Put on your collar and get down to the protests as quick as you can. They won't beat up a priest. We're trying to keep these kids from being killed!" He went.

Hubert Humphrey, who deplored the mayhem going on outside, finally won the Democratic nomination for president. Reams of paper and buckets of ink have been used in writing the history of this election. I spent a good bit of time trying to explain it to my students, and I wound up asking them to think about the turbulent events of 1968 and Humphrey's dilemma. He was still LBJ's vice president. Voters were sick and tired of the Vietnam War. But how could Humphrey campaign on an end-the-war plan without making LBJ look bad? He finally did, in September 1968, but it was too late. The election was in November.

Humphrey's Republican opponent was—you know who— Richard M. Nixon. Guess who won? Nixon ran again in 1972, and guess what happened next? Watergate. Think about what might have been, I would tell my students.

High spots of the 1960s have to include another "where were you when—" the Moon landing, July 20, 1969. We had had a government agency called the National Aeronautics and Space Administration (NASA) since 1958, but the Space Program began in earnest after Russia put a man into orbit in 1961. That year President Kennedy announced his goal was for the US to put a man on the moon "before this decade is out."

We did, but JFK didn't live to see it. He did see the Manned Spacecraft Center set up in 1961. Now it is known as he Lyndon B.

Johnson Space Center, in Clear Lake, Texas, about forty miles from Houston. Astronauts and their families moved there, and astronauts became mini-celebrities. The six pre-school children in our weekly playgroup were impressed because one of their fathers was an astronaut in training. He had not yet been assigned to a mission, but they were wowed, anyway. The astronaut's son became a playgroup celebrity. All of them learned about the space program called Apollo 1 that was aiming to fly men to the moon.

At 6:30 one morning, our phone rang. I was already in the kitchen making coffee, so I grabbed the wall phone. I will always remember answering that phone mounted on our bright yellow wall, and thinking what a dark message I heard. The caller was a playgroup mother. "No playgroup today," she said. "Bev (the astronaut's wife, that week's playgroup host) is going to Clear Lake to be with the wives."

"Hmmh?" I had not yet had coffee.

"Haven't you heard? There was a flash fire in the capsule late yesterday, and Grissom and White and Chafee are dead."

Another occasion for national mourning: Apollo I, the first phase of the moon landing program, had literally gone up in smoke on January 27, 1967. So had the lives of Edward (Gus) Grissom, Ed White, and Roger Chafee, three young astronauts in their prime.

Two years later, on July 20, 1969, Apollo 11 made it to the moon. Millions of people all over the world watched as Neil Armstrong, Edward (Buzz) Aldrin, and Michael Collins took off for the moon, and Armstrong and Aldrin became the first men to set foot on the lunar surface. If you don't know what Armstrong's famous quote was, look it up.

Where was I on that historic Sunday night? Our children, who were then ages six, five, and three (we had added daughter Anne as company for Catherine and Paul), have never let us forget that they watched the moon landing with their babysitter. Jim and I were at a moon-watch party. Ah, well.

When the moon astronauts returned to earth, they had to go into a quarantine for three weeks, lest they bring back a "moon plague." During that time, Marlene Dietrich was doing a concert date in Houston.

She wanted pictures of the astronauts for her grandsons. My husband, who was presenting her concert, suggested a trip to visit their wives, since the astronauts were still in quarantine. Jim drove her to Clear Lake, where she was to have tea with the wives. She carried some signed photos of herself to give them in exchange for photos of their husbands. When Jim came to take her back to Houston, she flounced into the car and said, looking at the modest bungalow on a street of similar ones, "How can they go to the moon—and come back—to this!" She had the astronauts' photos, but she still carried the envelope with her own photographs. "Miss Dietrich, you forgot to give them your pictures," Jim said.

"They didn't ask!" she snapped.

Those are my memories of the moon landing. Little did we know that another history-changing event had taken place the day before it. Sometime after midnight Friday and one o'clock Saturday morning, July 19, 1969, Senator Edward Kennedy drove off a bridge on an island called Chappaquiddick, Maine, and his passenger, a young woman names Mary Jo Kopechne, drowned inside the car. Kennedy swam free and did not report the accident until late Saturday morning. He did not explain his behavior to the public until a televised speech a week later. Many people did not believe him. What happened that fateful night is not quite clear to this day. There are books and movies, if you want to pursue it.

When I told my my students about this, I added my own story: Some years later Jim and I were visiting in Edgartown on Martha's Vineyard. Edgartown is where you take the ferry to Chappaquidick Island. A friend gave us what he called the Chappaquiddick tour. We saw the house where Ted Kennedy had partied. We drove along the road that Ted and Mary Jo had taken late that night after the party. Ted Kennedy's story was that, as he was heading for the ferry (the only way back to Martha's Vineyard), he did not realize he had taken a wrong turn in the dark, and his car went off the bridge and into a pond. But that "wrong turn" is a sharp right, not one you'd make by mistake. It is also a hard right turn onto a gravel road. If you are driving on a blacktop surface and suddenly turn onto gravel, you would know the difference, right? I think about that to this very day.

Another what-might-have been: Ted Kennedy was the youngest and the last of four Kennedy brothers. Three had died violent deaths: JFK and RFK downed by assassins' bullets; Joseph Kennedy Jr., the eldest brother, died when his plane went down in World War II. In the 1960s Ted Kennedy held a high pace in the nation's hearts—until Chappaquiddick. He was charged with leaving the scene of an accident and given a two-month suspended sentence. No one really knows what happened that fateful night, but Senator Ted Kennedy's image was tarnished. He earned respect for his later Senate career, but he might have gone higher, were it not for one night in 1969.

~

6. Woodstock, a monumental outdoor music festival in 1969, turned disastrous when 400,000 people showed up.

At the end of the Sixties was Woodstock. That name rings bells with thousands of people even today. From August 15 to 18,1969 it was near the site Max Yasgur's dairy farm in Bethel, a little town in upsgtate New York, where a rock music festival rocked the nation. You know the music. Every major artist, every top group, made the scene. You may even have been there, or you know somebody who was there. My where-were-you-when moment: I did not make Woodstock. In August 1969 Jim and I were in Houston with three children ages 7, 6, and 4, and a cat of indeterminate age. I was studying to finish my Ph.D. at Rice. Like the rest of America, we watched Woodstock on TV. Amid all the turmoil of the Sixties, the Woodstock Music and Arts Fair was to be a late summer festival of "Peace and Love." Fifty thousand people were expected. Four hundred thousand showed up. There will be riots, people said. There will be drugs and sex orgies. There were many worst-possible scenarios. What actually happened was a near miracle. Hundreds of thousands of young people camped out in rain and mud for three days, as music from major rock groups and stars played on, and on. The campers sang and danced. They shared food and joints (yes, Virginia, there was marijuana). The Woodstock festival sent a message of hope to a troubled nation. Watch the documentaries. Play the songs. Jimi Hendrix's "Star Spangled Banner" will tell you how much discord there was in the U.S.A.

A resilient nation had barely recovered from the turmoil of the Sixties when the political crisis known as "Watergate" threatened to undo us. For those too young to remember it, that name came from the Water Gate, once the site of symphony concerts on the banks of the Potomac River in Washington, D.C. A luxury hotel/apartment/office complex nearby was named "Watergate."

That innocent label became forever stained after the events of 1972-1974.

~

7. President Richard M. Nixon was impeached in 1974.

The year 1972 was a presidential election year. Richard Nixon wanted to make sure he was re-elected. For that purpose he had organized a fund-raising group called the Committee to Re-elect the President, known as CRP. Nixon's political enemies soon dubbed it CREEP. (I am not making this up. This was long before Radiohead's 1992 album, Creep, with a song of the same name that had nothing to do with politics.) In 1972 the wearisome, seemingly endless, war in Vietnam dragged on. America was a nation divided, (Sound familiar?) still split into pro-and anti-war factions. Nixon's Democratic opponent was George McGovern, a South Dakota senator. (My three children have never let me forget that when McGovern held a campaign rally in Houston I made them all go. They were then ages ten, nine, and seven. I knew the audience was going to be pitifully sparse, and McGovern needed all the help he could get.)

Nixon won.

And now, the Watergate timeline:

(Note: This is to show you how long it took to remove a President from power.)

(Another note: what follows here is just the bare bones of Watergate. If you want the red meat, look it up. Read the books. Watch the movies.)

June 17, 1972: In the summer before the November election, five men were arrested for burglary, for breaking into the Democratic National Committee's headquarters in the Watergate. Turns out, they were from CREEP.

Nixon said he knew nothing about it. Turns out, he was wrong.

January 3,1973: the Watergate burglars' trials began.

Nixon said he knew nothing about any of this. Turns out, he was wrong.

More damaging evidence came to light. Months went by. A special prosecutor was appointed.

October 20, 1973: Nixon ordered his attorney general to fire the special prosecutor. The attorney general refused, and resigned. Then Nixon ordered the deputy attorney general to do the firing. The deputy attorney general also refused and resigned. Nixon then ordered the solicitor general to do the firing, and he did. This breaking news was known as the "Saturday Night Massacre." I remember being at a dinner party when the news of this came, and everybody there was so upset we all scrapped the party and rushed home to hunker down in front of our own TV sets.

Ten days later, the wheels began to roll, soon to be followed by some heads.

October 30, 1973: the House of Representatives started an impeachment inquiry. These wheels turned very slowly, but news traveled very fast. Back then, most Americans were not sure what the word "impeachment" meant. (Who'd have thought that word would get so much use later on?) Many people back then though "impeachment" meant removal from office. When they were asked, "Do you think the President should be impeached" many said, "No." I was a young professor then, and I remember being asked to do a radio talk show interview, where I explained that the word "impeachment" means a trial, not a removal from office. If the trial finds the accused guilty, then the guilty party must go.

November 17, 1973: Nixon said, "I am not a crook."

Incriminating evidence was piling up.

February 6, 1974: the House Judiciary Committee formally began its impeachment investigation of President Richard Nixon. (Note how slowly the wheels turned.) More months went by.

May 9, 1974: President Richard Milhous Nixon was accused of
1. obstruction of justice
2. abuse of power   ]
3. contempt of Congress

That was a long, hot summer, especially for Republicans. But back then the members of that party could all agree on some things—like Richard Nixon's guilt. (Today's Republicans, please, please take note.)

August 8, 1974. President Richard Nixon, not wanting to be the second president since Andrew Johnson in 1868 to go through an impeachment trial, resigned as the 37th President of the United States.

Vice President Gerald Ford, the earnest, modest man who succeeded Nixon as president ("I'm a Ford, not a Lincoln."), gave his former boss a full unconditional pardon.

And, oh yes, the Vietnam War ended in 1975. We did not win it. We lost over 58,000 lives trying. It was a bitter, unpopular war. No welcome-home parades. Many young men who had fought there came home depressed. One of my students, when we talked about this, said, "My husband fought in Vietnam. When he came home, he had a drug problem and slept with a loaded pistol under his pillow. We are now divorced."

When the war ended, North Vietnam pushed southward and spread Communism over South Vietnam. See the musical. Read the books. Watch the documentaries and the movies. That reminds me of "Hearts and Minds," a powerful documentary about American soldiers in Vietnam that won an Oscar in 1975 for Best Documentary Feature. A colleague and I took a group of students to see it one night, and came back to my house to have coffee and discuss it. One graphic scene is a soldier and a prostitute in a Saigon brothel. The first thing our students (who were, as it happened, all males) said was, "We were so embarrassed to be there with you! It was like going to a sex movie with your mother! Why didn't you warn us?" My colleague and I, two middle-aged females, looked sheepish. "Sorry," we said.

After the war, thousands of South Vietnamese war refugees, "boat people," fled to the United States and other countries. Many came to Houston. Some of their children came to the University of St. Thomas. Some of them took my U.S. History Since 1877. Through the 80s and 90s, when we got to the Vietnam War, I would look over the class of about thirty, knowing there were 3 or 4 Vietnamese students among them. Then I would say, I know that some of you have memories of this, and if you can share them with us, we'd be really glad to hear. But they always sat silent, heads bowed, as if they wanted to crawl under their seats.

More years passed. Not until the early 2000s did any Vietnamese students volunteer to share their memories in class. These were the second generation, the children of those who had sat with heads down in my earlier classes. In 2006 I assigned an oral history project, to interview someone about memories of any war. There were half a dozen Vietnamese students in that freshman class. When students presented summaries of their projects for the whole class, the Vietnamese students, every one, had chosen—guess what?—the Vietnamese War. They had interviewed their parents and grandparents, some of whom still spoke nothing but Vietnamese. When the reports were finished, the rest of the class, along with the professor, burst into applause. We had heard things like this:

"There were dead bodies on the streets, and my family use to go out after dark and bury them. It was not dignified to leave them there."

"My family left in one of the last boats. It was really overloaded, and they feared it might sink. My grandmother was nine months pregnant with twins. It was very scary for them, but they made it. One of the twins was my mother."

"My grandfather was a colonel in the army. Viet Cong sent him to a camp. He was there a long time before he could get out and come to America."

I wish I had made copies of every one of those reports. Instead, like the proverbial absent-minded professor, I graded them and handed them back to their authors. What was I thinking of?

~

8. The very first computers were hand-held devices, as tiny as transistor radios.

The end of the Vietnam War came at the beginning of a momentous technological revolution, with new inventions replacing old ones, as the automobile had replaced the horse, and the incandescent light bulb, the oil lamp. On my university campus this revolution began in the 1970s, when some professors who taught math and physics began to enter student data on mysterious little punch-cards they fed into odd-looking machines, hoping to sort the cards with little holes and simplify the registration of thousands of students at the beginning of each term. Sometimes the little cards worked, and sometimes they screwed up.

It was about that time that phone systems with new bells and whistles—voice mail and conference calls and call forwarding—came into use. Our faculty had classes to learn how to use these multi-keyed phones, but not everybody was a fast learner. In a call to reach a history professor at Harvard, I was gratified to hear that even the Harvard history department was not phone-savvy: I could hear a secretary shouting down the hall, "Dr. Wood, you have a phone call!" and other voices yelling back, "He's not here!"

In 1984 while I was reading exams at the Advanced Placement US History readings I first made a phone call on something called a "cell phone." It was bigger and heavier than a flashlight, and a colleague at the exam readings wore it proudly clipped to his belt. He generously loaned it to as many as could use it, while the others lined up every night to call home on the phones in the dormitories that housed 300 exam readers. In those days a few people had something called a car phone, but those were few and far between. I knew of only one, given to a friend of mine by her husband, who also gave her a Jaguar.

Years later, Jim gave me a cell phone when I was teaching night classes at UST, in case I had car trouble coming home. I never used it.

While I was away reading AP U.S. history exams (which I did for two weeks every June from 1983 to 1995). Jim coped with three teenage children and an elderly cat and dog. As a consolation present for while I was gone, one summer I gave him something new, a gadget called a "Walkman," a pocket-sized transistor radio with earphones. It also played cassette tapes. He liked to take walks, so I figured it would amuse him. It did. Long before iPods, and way long before smartphones, people were seen in public wearing earbuds, cords dangling from their ears, listening to their own music on sidewalks, in stores, on buses, in airports. We still have that Walkman in the kitchen drawer in case we need an extra battery-powered radio if there's a hurricane.

Although nobody realized it at the time, the Age of the Computer had already begun. In those long-gone days the word "computer" meant an enormous machine as big as a garage. The capacities of such monsters were beyond imagination. We had seen "Hal" in the 1968 movie, *2001*, and were suitably awed. Then one day our son Paul came home and said, "Robert has a computer in his house." We thought he was joking. "No, really. It's on his dad's desk." Robert's father was a professor of engineering at Rice, yes, but still we were skeptical.

[The following discussion of computers is limited and one-sided, based solely on the recollections and practical applications of one who barely passed freshman calculus and never took physics. If you want scientific explanations, skip this part.]

One day in the late 1970s a colleague of mine at the University of St. Thomas told me that a friend of his who worked for a big oil firm had a new machine in her office called a "word processor."

"It's amazing," he said. "It's like a typewriter with a screen above it, and it puts the words on the screen so you can correct typos, and add or take out words, and then you can print out the final copy." Who had ever heard of such a thing? In those days most documents and letters were done on a typewriter with carbons for copies. If you were lucky you had a giant IBM Correcting Selectric, which had keys that corrected your typing errors right there on the page. If you didn't have a Correcting Selectric, you could use paper called "corrasable bond," a thin, slick, sleazy paper that let you use a plain pencil eraser to rub out mistakes. Or you used regular paper and a little bottle of a white solution called "Liquid Paper" to paint over your typos with a tiny brush, blew on the page to dry it, and then typed over your errors. Even so, a good typist was still worth her (they were always female) weight in gold. I worked with one in my first job. She could type for pages and pages, single-spaced and error-free, with three or four carbon copies. On the rare times she made an error and had to correct the original and all its copies, she uttered (under her breath, of course) words that would make most foul-mouthed sailor blush. Most people who made typing errors used Liquid Paper. Invented by a Bette Nesmith Graham, a typist, who mixed up the first batches in her kitchen in 1951, it made her a rich woman by the 1960s. Office workers and students and teachers and anybody who used a typewriter used gallons of Liquid Paper.

For people who made their livings by putting words and numbers on paper, the "word processor" was as revolutionary as Gutenberg's printing press. After the word processor, the rest was history. Goodbye, carbon paper, goodbye, flimsy onion-skin copies, goodbye, Liquid Paper. And goodbye, endless re-typing of pages every time you revised a manuscript and inserted a phrase or a footnote. The first printers that connected to word processors were spool-fed contraptions that printed on a roll of paper with perforated edges that fitted on sprockets. When your print job rolled out, you carefully ripped off the perforated edges with the holes, tore the pages apart, and there you had—well, a readable, usable, if not elegant, document.

My first computer was an Apple IIc, which I got in 1985. It was "notebook-sized"—that is, if you wanted a notebook that weighed nearly eight pounds—plus its monitor and cables, another eight or ten pounds. It had no hard drive (who ever heard of such a thing?) and no memory to speak of. You put in a start-up disk into the computer's tummy each time you used it and went from there. Your documents could be stored on other disks called "floppies." In the summer of 1985 I took my computer with me on a research trip to Bermuda, lugging it in my briefcase, with its cumbersome monitor stowed in my carry-on bag. Airport security? Nobody even asked me to open my bags.

In 2001, when we moved out of our old house, I found a stack of old floppies with my 1000-page novel on them. The program that created them was ancient history, and so, I reasoned, were they. My historical novel, *A Durable Fire*, was already in print (William Morrow, 1990). So I threw away the only digital copy of that manuscript. Bad move: years later, when my novel was reissued, I had to pay a hefty sum to have the hard copy scanned for the reprint.

The moral of this tale: Don't throw away old disks, LP records, or cassette tapes, or CD's, or cameras that use film, or typewriters that use ribbons.

You just never know.

The 1980s were also the beginning of the Age of the Internet: For desk-top computers the first connections were primitive. At least, most at-home connections were. I plugged a cord into my computer's backside, and that cord that snaked around the corner of my desk, into the hallway, and finally into the kitchen, to plug into a phone jack. This was the dial-up era. To get on "The Internet" you turned on your computer, selected one of several phone numbers, clicked on it, and waited: Mysterious noises--static and growls and roars--issued forth, and then, with patience and luck, you were on the "Internet Highway." If a thunderstorm occurred while you were dialed in ("online" was a term not yet used) you quickly pulled out the cord from the phone jack, lest a random lightning bolt come through it and fry your computer.

In those days the "World Wide Web," (a term coined in 1974, better known as "www," needed web addresses: long strings of mysterious letters and symbols that you keyed into a box on your screen, hit "Enter" and hoped something appeared. In those first (pre-search engine and pre-Google) years, web addresses were essential. For a while there were Internet directories: thick telephone-book-sized volumes published for various subjects. The History Department at the University of St. Thomas had one for history websites. Amazed, we shared its contents ("Look! Here's one for the Civil War!") with each other, and with awe-struck students. Web addresses were like precious jewels, to be treasured and given out sparingly. If a student found one that worked for a class topic (the Gilded Age, for example) he or she wrote its long web address (url) laboriously on the blackboard, and the rest of us painstakingly copied it into our notebooks.

Our university reference librarian, a bright young man in his early thirties, was our source of all information about The Web and its wonders. I remember one afternoon he said to me, with a look of rapture on his face, his eyes shining behind his glasses, "Some day all the knowledge in the world will be available online."

He was not far wrong.

Back then, the Web and email and all their myriad uses were still unknown, but we learned fast. One new use was emails to my classes. With a digital camera the size of an obese fountain pen, I snapped pictures of all of my students on the first day of class. "I'm going to come around and take your picture, if you're OK with that. Then I'll email it to you and you can send it to your parents, and say, 'See, here I am in history class.'" They were highly amused.

Then there came something called a "fax," a new wonder that could transmit documents over a telephone line to a desktop machine that spewed forth printed, albeit flimsy, copies. That meant you could dial a fax number to almost anywhere, hit a key, and send your document instantly. One of my students asked me if he could fax his term paper to me to meet the deadline, since he would be out of town on a business trip. I said of course, and gave him our history department fax number. On the day those papers were due, there was no fax from my student. Later that afternoon I had a phone call from a watch repair shop nearby. "We just got an eighteen-page fax that looks like a history term paper," an irritated voice said. As it turned out, it was: my student had mis-copied the fax phone number.

"I'll come by and pick it up," I said.

By now you may have noticed that this book is not an outline of U.S. history, or of presidential administrations, or even of politics. It hits what I consider the high spots. You may have others, but these are mine. The Age of the Computer brought undreamed-of changes, but we can't leave the last few decades without mentioning two other things that changed people's lives. One of them was Roe v. Wade, recently in the news in our own time. That earth-trembling event was a Supreme Court decision in 1973 that made abortion legal and therefore safe. That meant that if a pregnant woman wanted not to have the baby, she had was free to choose abortion. Many, many people were glad, and many, many people were sad. Right to Life went toe-to-toe with Planned Parenthood. I had not been teaching very long when Roe v. Wade was a major news item. I used to tell my students that abortion was a dangerous issue. It encouraged single-issue politics. It could become like slavery in another century, and single-issue politics could be very dangerous for all parties. It made many people decide which candidate to vote for, depending on their stand on one single issue. As a professor in a Catholic university, I had to tiptoe very carefully around this one.

Some years later I taught a course called "The History of the American Family" that included the history of birth control as well as abortion. One day, as I talked about unwed motherhood, which was for much of U.S. history a terrible disgrace, I said something about some families in the old days sending a pregnant daughter away for the duration, to hide the shame. As I spoke, a young woman in that class looked down at her middle and folded her hands. As months went by, her middle grew larger and larger. Then she stopped attending class. I later learned that she was from Massachusetts, and that her family had sent her to spend a semester (and her pregnancy) at UST. After all, we were a Catholic university.

Another thing that stands out in my teaching memory of the Seventies and the Eighties is AIDS (Aquired Immune Deficiency Syndrome). We first heard of it at the beginning of the 1980s. AIDS, like abortion, was a delicate subject. I knew young men who had it. I knew people who knew people who had it. I knew young men who died of it. AIDS was a death sentence in those days. One day a student came to my office. He had been absent more often than present in my class.

"I wanted to come and see you. I know I've missed a lot of classes," he said. He was so pale and thin, he looked like a breath could blow him away.

"Sit down," I said.

His sad brown eyes met mine, and he said, "I have AIDS."

"I'm so sorry." I said. I hated those trite words as soon as they came out of my mouth. Then I said, "Let me know if I can help." He and I both knew that nobody could help him, but I didn't know what else to say. In those days AIDS was a death sentence. Nowadays it is treatable, and people who have it live out their lives.

On another front, the nation began to think about sexual harassment. The live TV coverage of hearings to confirm Clarence Thomas as a Supreme Court judge in 1991 was better than a soap opera.

A star witness, attorney Anita Hill, accused him of sexual harassment. (We won't go into the lurid details here.) And, oh, yes: both of them were Black. When all was said and done, Clarence Thomas took his seat on the U.S. Supreme Court, where he remains to this day. He is married to a white woman. Anita Hill is a professor of law at Brandeis University.

A federal law in 1991 gave women the right to sue if they could prove sexual harassment. That was a trendy (i.e., sexy) topic for a national conversation, and a good opener at many a cocktail party . Those were innocent days. A male student of mine walked into my office one morning and said, "I'd like to tell you that's a really nice dress you're wearing—but I'd better not!" We both laughed.

Since then there have been many national conversations, many involving prominent men, including two Presidents, about various sexual harassment charges. The "Me, too" movement began in 2006 and grew and grew, as more and more women went public about what men had done to them, or with them. The list of them is too long for this book.

We are tactfully skipping over the story of William Henry Clinton and Monica and the cigar and the blue dress, and the first presidential impeachment trial since Andrew Johnson's in 1868. I was glad not to have to teach it. In my day the U.S survey class barely had time to get past the Sixties by the end of the spring semester. I did not have to teach about the Gulf War or the Iraq War, either, but when the Gulf War broke out in 1991 I shared the fears of countless mothers who had sons in the military who could soon be "in harm's way." Our son Paul was then a lieutenant in the U.S. Naval Reserve, living in California.

If you want details of the Gulf War in brief: Iraqi forces, steered by Saddam Hussein, president of Iraq, invaded and annexed Iraq's oil-rich neighbor, Kuwait.

Here's a part of my 1991 diary:

Jan. 7 Will the world go to war this year--50 years after this country entered WW II? Will it be Armageddon? I begin to hear war drums beat.

Jan. 8 And then the news—preparations for war in the VA [Veterans Administration] hospital! Dear God. The deadly countdown to Jan. 15 goes on.

Jan. 10 Will the 20th century end with an awful bang?

Jan. 15 The Persian Gulf deadline hangs over everything. Will there be, after all this saber-rattling, a miracle?

Jan. 16 War. It began at 6 p.m. with news on CNN of "flashes in the sky over Baghdad." Watched with grisly fascination as reports of fantastic UN-US air attacks. Almost too good to be true. Went to bed at 12, wondering what the retaliation will be. Dear God, let this be short. Talked to Paul who wishes he were there.

[On that January night I was having dinner at a friend's house. At happy hour we turned on CNN to catch the news, and quickly set down our wine glasses. "Flashes over Baghdad," bursts of orange and yellow against a black sky, were filling the TV screen. The war was on: We watched in horror as bombs exploded in real time. We had planned to go to a Book-and-Author (yours truly being one of the authors) event at Rice University that evening, but I looked at my friend and said, "I'm not going." She said OK. I called to cancel, and learned that Rice had already cancelled the event in light of the war news.]

Jan. 17 This terrible war-while-you-watch coverage is gripping and frightening and saddening. At bedtime the new terror came, w/more missiles on Israel (and promises of "unknown terrorists" entering the US. Paul called home to get Jim's office phone number. He musters Saturday. Is told to be ready to leave on 24 hours' notice. God forbid.

Jan. 19 Newspaper carries matter-of-fact piece on "Air Travel in Wartime." Drugstore has little flag pins on a board that says "Remember Our Troops."

Jan. 22. War news blackens: oil fires now burning in Kuwait .

Jan. 23. War a week old, more ominous every day.

Jan. 25 War worsens--now oil slick, huge and horrid, creeps over Persian Gulf!
. . .
[The End: A coalition of United Nations forces led by the United States, drove Iraqi forces out of Kuwait in a mercifully short conflict.]

Feb. 27 Watched war end: 95 US casualties. Bush's short speech not bad. Unbelievable capitulation by the Evil One [Saddam Hussein]. It is too good to be true. Poor Vietnam vets, who now must see a welcome home for Gulf War troops and watch a <u>win</u> they never had.

Saddam Hussein withdrew, very disgruntled. A few years later he would cause more trouble for another President Bush.

The second Bush was George H. W.'s son and heir, George W., then the Republican governor of Texas, who won the disputed election of 2000.

Given the current state of national politics, and the number of people who still believe in the Big Steal of 2020, this 2000 election is worth a closer look.

On election night, November 7, 2000, as a nation eagerly watched the vote counts on TV, it looked as if George W. Bush (the son) had won. Democrat Al Gore, then Clinton's vice president, called Bush and congratulated him. Then, an hour later, Gore called back and said, in so many words, Whoa. There were votes still uncounted in Florida, and that could decide the election. This was not good news for anybody.

Days, then weeks. of legal wrangling, nail-biting suspense. Florida was doing a manual recount of votes in four counties. But on December 12 the U.S. Supreme Court, in a 5-4 decision, nixed the manual recount and declared Bush the winner. I remember getting the news on campus that Tuesday: As I walked back to my office in the History House after class, the entire faculties of History and Political Science were on the front porch, looking like somebody had just died. "It's over," somebody said. "They gave it to Bush," said another. Bush came out with 271 Electoral College votes to Gore's 266. But Gore won the popular vote by more than half a million: 50,999,897 to Bush's 50,456,002.

Under our antiquated electoral college system, Bush the Son got the win. Democrats, especially Al Gore, took that loss bravely. Gore could have sulked and said Bush's win was a Big Steal, but he didn't. As a result, the political kettle went from boil back to its usual simmer, and Gore's followers never tried to attack the Capitol. (Republicans today could learn something here.) Thus ended the Election of 2000. Note: Bush the Younger's political enemies came to call him "Shrub." Think about it.

The twentieth century ended, for most of us, not in 1999, and not in 2000, but on September 11, 2001, known ever after as "9/11." Talk about a "where-were-you-when" moment. I was in the kitchen, putting slices of bread in the toaster, thinking about my 9:35 a.m. colonial history class, when the phone rang. Our friend Dorothy, a former journalist who faithfully watched morning TV, always called us when something big happened. She knew we would have our heads buried in newspapers at breakfast.

"Turn on your TV," she said. "A plane has just hit one of the World Trade buildings." This was just after 7:46 a.m. CST, or 8:46 a.m. New York, EST.

I thanked Dorothy, but I was only mildly concerned. I remembered a time when I was in graduate school and a plane had hit a tall building in New York. That was scary, but not earth-shaking, especially if you were in Philadelphia. Now I switched on the little TV in the kitchen, which was reporting a plane crashing into the North Tower of the World Trade Center. Probably a small plane off course, I said to myself, and hopefully not much damage done. But I called out to Jim, who put down his paper and came to see. As he walked into the kitchen, the TV picture showed another plane—a big one— hitting the South Tower. Struck dumb by horror and disbelief, we watched it burst into smoke and flames,. In a few minutes the news broadcast suddenly changed to Washington, D.C. A plane had just crashed into the Pentagon. More smoke and flames filled our little TV screen.

"Are we in a Tom Clancy movie?" I said, clutching Jim's arm. It was now a few minutes after 8:37 a.m. by our clocks. Jim looked at me and said, "Nothing will ever be the same again."

How right he was.

The clock was ticking. I mechanically prepared to go to the campus and meet my 9:35 class. Jim, whose arts-management job had no time clock, went to his office as usual. What else could we do?

I drove to the campus, wondering how the sky could be so blue, the sun so bright, on such a black day. Everything looked perfectly normal. As I walked across the academic quadrangle, I met a political science professor running back to his office. "South Tower's just collapsed!" He shouted at me, panting, and kept running, as if he were going to do something to put a stop to all of this. I kept walking.

Most of my students were sitting in their seats, waiting for me, looking scared. This was an upper-division history class, and it had a dozen juniors and seniors. I didn't even put my briefcase down.

"I don't know about you," I said, "but I don't feel much like talking about Anne Hutchinson and John Winthrop today. Let's go watch the big TV in the student center." So we trooped across the quad and settled down, along with a crowd of students and faculty already there, in front of the giant TV. As I recall, nobody spoke. There were not enough chairs for such a crowd, and we latecomers sat on the floor and watched more unbelievable footage: yet another plane had crashed in a field near Shanksville, in Somerset County, Pennsylvania. That was the now-famous Flight 93, bound for San Francisco, but aimed to hit Washington, D.C. Undaunted, daring passengers confronted hijackers, causing them to crash the plane, killing all aboard. We heard from President George W. Bush, filmed from a classroom full of elementary-schoolers he was visiting in

Florida. Looking startled, like a possum caught in a flashlight's beam, he told the nation that this was likely a "terrorist attack." Then we saw the North Tower collapse.

The rest of that day had a surreal quality. Our campus held its regular noontime Mass, but with a special liturgy, "Mass in Time of War." The chapel was full. Afterward I kept a lunch date with a colleague at a Chinese restaurant. "We might as well have a good lunch," he said, "We may need to keep up our strength."

Around us, Houston's downtown skyscrapers were closed. Offices were empty. Air travel across the U.S. was grounded. A terrified nation wondered if more attacks were to come. What had already come was terrible enough.

We would eventually learn that nearly3,000 people had been killed, and another 6,000 injured. September 11, 2001 was the worst terrorist attack in history. Across the globe, much of the world mourned with us, held candlelight vigils, prayer services. At home, a national grief engulfed us. TV news, nightmarish day after day, replayed footage of the Twin Towers collapsing. That was maybe the last time all Americans felt as one.

On September 20, nine days after 9/11, Jim and I flew to New York City for a convention. The annual meeting of the National Alliance for Musical Theatre had decided not to cancel, and New York was very glad to see us. Mayor Rudy Guiliani thanked everybody who came. Guiliani's political career has since had a downside, but back then was "America's Mayor," a model of compassion and leadership.

We flew to New York on a plane that was eerily empty, about twenty of us in a cabin that seated 200. Airplanes by then had gone back to flying, but people had not. Here are the notes I made in my diary for that trip.

In the taxi from the airport to our hotel, Jim asked the driver if things were getting back to normal.

"No." I had never heard such sorrow in one syllable. We passed a US flag, grimy with ashes and smoke from the tower fires, fluttering bravely from a lopsided pole on a thru-way barrier.

In the hotel elevator:

A fireman from Chicago, grim and weary-looking, red backpack on his shoulder, going back for another shift in the wreckage. He told us they were switching from search-and-rescue to "demolition stage" the next day. This was Thursday, September 20. Nine days of feverish, frantic searching, and no survivors in the mountains of twisted steel and concrete. "Demolition stage." I have seldom heard such sorrow in a voice.

Another fireman, this one from San Diego, with the same sad eyes, which were at odds with his bright-blue uniform. I marvelled at so many who had come from across the U.S. to help. Our midtown Manhattan hotel was full of them—and of New Yorkers who had fled their apartments near the Twin Towers.

A young man clutching his cellphone said, "I saw it all." He told us he lived two blocks from the World Trade Center. "The worst part was the bodies falling." The horror was still in his eyes. I didn't want to think about what he saw. He and his three eighty-pound dogs had come to stay at our hotel. "They've been very good to us," he said.

At dinner at Sofia's [one of our favorite New York restaurants]: On a big TV screen, the news, with President Bush addressing the nation. Every table in that restaurant fell to silent attention—all but one table. I turned around to glare at the noisy ones, and Jim said, "That's their right. This is a free country."

On the streets of Manhattan:

U.S. flags were everywhere. On buildings, hung outside like curtains. On lapels. On cars, flying from antennas. Blooming in jars on counters, like little bouquets of patriotism.

On a wall outside St. Vincent's Hospital, at 203 West 12th Street, there were hundreds of photographs and names, with signs saying things like Have you seen me? Call--- and a phone number.

St.Vincent's was the closest trauma center to the World Trade Center, and on the morning of 9/11 the trauma staff had quickly geared up, ready for the onslaught of injured victims they thought would come. They waited and waited all day and into the night in vain. Instead, they soon had a wall of names. So many missing, so many loved ones gone up in ashes.When we were there the smoky, scorchy, dusty smell still lingered. It would be there for weeks. Our son Paul (who by then was a museum exhibit designer) told me to buy some souvenirs of the Twin Towers while they were still available. I bought a stack of touristy postcards of the Towers, the kind that are ten for a dollar. I gave them to my students, some of whom, I heard later, had sold them for a pretty penny on E-Bay. I also bought a little statuette of the Towers, which I still have on my desk.

After 9/11, my husband was right when he said, "nothing will ever be the same again." Fear had come off our TV screens and taken up residence with us, like an uninvited relative come to stay. We had suffered the worst terrorist attack in history. Would there be another? Was it "if" or "when"? That Christmas all three of our grown children came to spend it with us, in case this turned out to be our last family gathering. We gave them high-powered flashlight/searchlights as presents.

At this writing, there have been no more 9/11's. No more Black Hawk helicopters buzzing over Super Bowl stadiums. No more troops with high-powered rifles on rooftops, watching for snipers. Instead, more high-powered guns are shooting schoolchildren, moviegoers, concert attendees, shoppers, nightclubbers, and church and synagogue congregations, not to mention people on the streets. Gun control? Ha! We have more guns than people in this country. We have yet to get over our frontier heritage and agree on what the Second Amendment means. Here it is, in case you need to refresh your memory:

"A well regulated Militia, being necessary to the security of a free State, the right of the people to keep and bear Arms, shall not be infringed."

Some people believe that those words must forever mean exactly what the writers of the original (1789) U.S. Constitution meant by them.

.

Some people believe that our 233-year-old Constitution, written for a nation of nearly four million people who traveled on horseback, plowed with oxen, and burned wood for heat, must bend with the times.

Some people say we have national and state military forces to keep us safe, and private citizens do not need high-powered military-style weapons to defend themselves or hunt game.

Think about it.

So far, we can give twenty-first century a mixed review, at best.

We had another war in 2003, waged against Saddam Hussein and his alleged "weapons of mass destruction," but really to pay him back for his supposed complicity in 9/11. ("Weapons of mass destruction" turned out to be a fiction. We won't go into that here.) U.S. air and ground forces invaded Iraq on March 19 and 20, 2003. After was a short, but, as it turned out, not sweet, struggle, the U.S. forces came out winners: On May 1, 2003, President George W. Bush landed triumphantly on the deck of an aircraft carrier under a "Mission Accomplished" banner. He declared victory, but was he ever wrong! Saddam Hussein was captured, tried, and executed, but the war in Iraq slogged on for nearly nine more years. The last U.S. combat troops left Iraq in 2011.

In January 2009, Barack Hussein Obama took office as the first Black President of the United States.("Hussein" is Arabic for "handsome" or "good." His father was a Muslim.) Such a hopeful time that was! Obama and his wife, Michelle, and their two daughters, Malia and Sasha, were a fascinating new First Family. Much of the world, not just the United States, thought so, too. Obama got a Nobel Peace Prize before he had been in office a year. Not everybody in this country was thrilled. Racism, that skeleton in our national closet, fell out again. Barack Obama's two-term presidency (2008-2016) is too new to assess his place in history. You can read what both Obamas, husband and wife, thought about this historic era in their best-selling memoirs. You can also read about them in dozens of other books.

You can also read dozens of books about Obama's successor, in the White House, one Donald J. Trump. This book is not one of them.

The election of 2016–not to mention 2020— is still too hot to handle. It is probably safe to say that Trump's presidency plowed up the American political landscape. What seeds will grow out of that soil? We have no idea so far.

We know that Democrats and Republicans have split wider and wider, that our national politics is more fragmented that ever. And that our democracy is in a perilous place.

We know that on Donald Trump's watch, a deadly pandemic called Covid 19 spread across our country and across the globe, killing six million worldwide—so far. We know that President Trump told us it would all be over by Easter 2020. It wasn't. We know that people began to disagree on whether or not to wear a mask, and then whether or not to get vaccinated. Those disagreements are still dividing us.

Americans need to know their history, good and bad. Not to sound too preachy or school-marm-ish, but we may be in danger of losing part of that history. As a colleague said at a history conference years ago, at the beginning of the Internet Age, "The train has left the station—and most of us are not on it." What's on that train? A mind-numbing, ever-changing technology of information and news. "TMI" is text-speak for "too much information." Facebook. Twitter. Instagram. Tik Tok. That is not all. By the time you read this book, there will no doubt be lots of newer ones.

The times, as Bob Dylan's song said, are indeed "a'changin'.

"If you want to know my theory about changing times, I'll tell you what I used to tell my students. There are times in American history when a heap of changes fell on people's heads all at once.

Example 1: A generation after the Civil War, in the so-called Gilded Age. for example, (like the TV series named for it) the Industrial Age swung into high gear. There were trains that could travel over thirty miles an hour, faster than the human body had ever travelled. There were "horseless carriages" made horses rear and plunge when they saw one on the street, and newfangled inventions like the telephone (human voices carried over a wire), electric light (rooms flooded with light, no need to go to bed at dark) and the phonograph (recorded lullabies and love songs, critics said, would do away with live voices). With these came labor strikes, financial panics, and big businesses called "trusts."

I know about trusts: My great-uncle Dilwyn Varney Purington (you may remember him as the Civil War officer earlier in this book) went into the business of manufacturing bricks after the war. By the late 1890s and early 1900s he was making a fortune as president of the Purington Paving Brick Company. Dilwyn's younger brother, William, my grandfather, was the vice-president and general manager. Many a street in the Midwest was paved with bricks that had "Purington Paver" stamped on them. Purington bricks helped build the Panama Canal. When my husband heard this bit of family history, he looked at me and said, "So how come you're not a brick heiress?"

Well, it turns out that my great-uncle Dilwyn was one of what history later called "Robber Barons." These were big business tycoons who created monopolies that hurt small businesses. Standard Oil was one example. The Purington Paving Brick Company was another. The Sherman Anti-Trust Act of 1890 tried to put a stop to unfair practices, and in 1910 *United States v. Purington* accused that company of creating a monopoly of the paving brick business. Three years later the case was declared *nolle prosequi,* which means "will no longer prosecute." How come? That puzzle of family history is still missing some pieces. I aim to delve into it some day. All I know is that my grandfather resigned from Purington Paving in 1911 and took a position with a cement company in Des Moines, Iowa. His big brother Dilwyn cut him out of any share in the brick company and wrote him out of his will. Maybe there's a TV series here?

Example 2: In my theory of changing historical times, the next big one is the 1920s. That was the decade known as the "Roaring Twenties. (The 1890s were once known as the "Gay Nineties"—but that's not what you think. Until the 1960s, "gay" meant joyful, happy, cheerful, etc. Not homosexual. Not in the Twenties. Back then, that "h" word was not spoken. The Roaring Twenties was called that because after World War I the nation went into party mode: People were dancing to a shocking new kind of music called "jazz." Automobiles were now affordable, thanks to Henry Ford's modest Model T's. (That meant dating and petting and necking could get out of the front parlor or the porch swing!) Young women were bobbing their hair short, wearing skirts above their knees, and calling themselves "flappers." Moving pictures showed scandalous amounts of skin. And, oh, yes, there was Prohibition!

On January 19, 1919 the 18th Amendment to the U.S. Constitution cut off the "manufacture, sale and transport of alcoholic beverages."

Yes.

No drinking. Period. That was the law, but people found ways to get around it, and illegal hooch turned into a big business, making gangsters like Al Capone rich and famous. Other people made do with "bathtub gin," home brews, or drinking in "speakeasies," illegal bars where you had to know the password to get in. I know a bar in New York City that still sports a little sliding door in its front entrance, from the days when it was a speak-easy and you had to pass inspection and whisper the right word to be let in. Prohibition lasted until December 5, 1933, when the 21st Amendment repealed the 18th.

What possessed Americans to make drinking alcohol a crime? Partly the war: keep our boys sober and safe. Germans drink beer, so beer is bad. Rellgious crusades against "demon rum" and temperance movements had been around since the 1820s, and in the early 1900s a woman named Carrie Nation made her name smashing saloons with a hatchet.

Changing times in the Twenties also had to do with World War I, and the flu pandemic of 1918 (they called it the "Spanish flu" because news of it first came from Spain.) It started in May 1918 and lasted about 18 months, and killed as many as 20 million, maybe 50 million worldwide (data collecting was not very efficient in those days). That flu was worse than World War I, which killed about 17 million people. In the United States, the death toll from the flu was 675,000. (Our own 2020-and-counting Covid 19 pandemic has topped that number, getting close to a million as of March 2022, and we're not over it yet.) Oddly enough, American history books mostly ignored the 1918 flu, which killed lots more Americans than the 53,000 we lost in World War I. I mentioned the Spanish flu only in passing in my classes, and sometimes we looked at a documentary about it.In 2020 Covid gave historians a wakeup call, and more delving into the history of 1918's pandemic is in progress.

The war and the flu were only a part of the changing times in the Twenties. Besides getting over deaths and losses, Americans had to face a flood of immigrants Since the turn of the century millions of immigrants (sound familiar?) had moved to the United States. Most of these foreigners were, how shall we say—foreign-looking: they were dark-haired, olive-skinned people from southern and eastern Europe. Not the blond, blue-eyed, light-skinned models of what some people called One Hundred Percent American. And even worse, to many Protestant Americans, too many of these foreigners were Jews or Catholics. Besides them, more Black Americans were migrating to places outside the South. Cities everywhere were growing. America was becoming an urban nation, where more people lived in towns and cities than in rural areas. Farmers felt left out: too many new inventions, too many foreigners. Many people wished for a return to the "good old days." Today those people want to Make America Great Again. Same thing. Too much change, too many people feeling the times are passing them by. The train has left the station, and they are not on it.

~

9. Being "gay," (i.e. homosexual) has been socially OK since the "Gay Nineties (i.e., 1890s).

Since the Civil War, we've had the Gay Nineties, the Roaring Twenties, World War II, the Sixties—and after that, we don't really have catchy names for the next decades. We haven't even agreed on what to do about the enormous technological changes and social changes in our lifetimes. Speaking of social change, there is one elephant in the room: the LGBTQ issue. It is still uneasy-making for many people, and it has come about with breath-taking speed.

In case you have been hiding your head in the sand, its letters stand for Lesbian Gay Bisexual Transexual Queer. In the Fifties, when I was in college, "queer" meant homosexual. "Gay" still meant "joyful." We'd never even heard of "bisexual," which means a person who is attracted to both males and females. For "transexual," keep reading. By the Sixties all that changed. Historians are still trying to figure out why. There is no one day when it all happened, but the Stonewall riots of June 27-29, 1969 are one marker, now celebrated every year with Gay Pride parades and marches. Stonewall was the name of a bar in New York's Greenwich Village where homosexuals gathered. When police began to harass them, they finally protested. Across the U.S., gay people "came out." From the 1970s until the 2000s, homosexuality became less and less shocking—although still illegal.

Here's the breathtaking speed part: By 2003 consenting sex between two adults was legal, by 2010 homosexuals were OK in the military, and by 2015 marriage between two people of the same sex was legal. How's that for turning things upside down? Many people were glad, and many, many other people were sad, and many were beyond sad: they were angry and bewildered. Their world had changed beyond belief. But in recent years, there has been another unsettling change: transexuality has come out, too. Most people had never even heard that word. People whose gender identity (male or female) did not match their physical equipment are called transexual. Science now has ways to help them get it right. Drugs and surgery can transform a transexual into the person they want to be. That is not OK with some people, who have tried to make laws about who can use whose restrooms, who can play on sports teams (can a trans-male, biologically stronger, play as a female?) and lately, who can even get the medical treatment necessary for their sex change (a medical necessity, many doctors say).

The times are a'changin.' Faster than Bob Dylan ever dreamed.

How did we get here? That's not only because of all the rapid-fire changes in our society, it's because of the way we get our information about the world we live in. Some of us watch only Fox News. Millions of Americans—one recent poll says four out of ten people—are avid Fox News fans. About the same number—four out of ten—are not. That's eight out of ten, you say. What about the other two? Your guess is as good as anybody's. But Fox News, and that network's four other talk shows, are the top five in cable ratings. And what, you ask, is wrong with Fox News? Fox News, to put it politely, skews the news. Right-wing folks and Republicans love it. Wait a minute, you say, what about CNN? What about MSNBC? They are openly left-wing and fond of Democrats. True. But whatever happened to unbiased news coverage?

In the old days (I won't call them the good old days here, but I often think it) we had only three major TV networks: ABC (American Broadcasting Company), CBS (Columbia Broadcasting System) , and NBC (National Broadcasting Company). That was BC (Before Cable). Each major network had an evening news broadcast. (As a matter of fact, they still do, but only old people watch them. You can tell by their number of commercials for drugs for elderly folks.) In bygone days the nightly news was how most people learned what was going on. They trusted Walter Cronkite (CBS) Chet Huntley and David Brinkley (NBC) and Peter Jennings (ABC) and other newscasters to give it to them straight, to tell them the truth about current events. From the 1940s to the 1980s, that was mainly how the American public got its news about everything. We were all on the same diet. Then came cable TV. CNN, the first cable news network, appeared in 1980, and MSNBC in 1996, the same year as Fox News. The rest, as the old trite saying goes, is history. Make of it what you will.

If many people watch and read (some still read newspapers and magazines) only what they agree with, and never hear or see anything that disagrees or offers another point of view, how ignorant they will be! How can they live in their own one-sided world? How will they know what they're missing? And if children (let's call them K-12) and college students get to learn only things that will not upset them (no history of unpleasant topics like racism, bigotry, antisemitism, for instance), what kind of citizens will they be? Think on that.

Banning books like *Huckleberry Finn* and *Beloved* and *To Kill a Mockingbird* is not the way to go. Neither is cutting out parts of our history. (Review the ten true-false questions that began this book.)

~

10. Donald J. Trump really had enough votes to win the presidency in 2020.

The worst of all Fake News is that Donald Trump really won the 2020 presidential election and was done out of it by voter fraud, i.e. the Big Steal. Worse than that, Donald Trump himself still believes it. And even worse, many people still believe him. As   of late 2021, two-thirds of Republicans, or 67 percent, want Donald Trump to be a major figure in their party, and 44 percent want him to run again for President. They are Trump's "Base," a formidable chunk of political clout. Republican politicians who want to get re-elected go against Trump at their peril. Even after what happened on January 6, 2021. (Will that come to be known as 1/6, a calendar shorthand for a horrendous day that everybody will remember, like 9/11?) As of early 2022, trials are just beginning for some 750 accused culprits.

As for my "where-were-you moment, it is forever seared in my memory. Here is my diary for that day, Wednesday, January 6, 2021:

61 □□□ [These little symbols mean that the weather in Houston is 61 degrees and partly cloudy, and the two smiley faces are me and my husband, meaning this promises to be a good day. I was wrong.]A day that turned ugly: as Electoral College results tallied & rogue Republicans made their false case, Trump "patriots" as he called them, stormed the Capitol. Chaos. A woman shot. Congress evacuated. Police taken by surprise. Violent malevolent mob ruled the day till dark. Trump did nothing. His Twitter account shut off after a dangerous post. What will come of this? Can we get through the next two weeks? The next two weeks meant the time until Wednesday, January 20, when Joseph R. Biden was to be inaugurated as President of the United States.

On that fateful earlier Wednesday I had decided I would devote myself to watching live news coverage of a historic event: the meeting of Congress to certify the results of the Electoral College that declared Biden President. The Electors had tallied Biden's 306 votes to Trump's 232. (To be President, you needed 270.) Biden had already won 81,268,924 popular votes to Trump's 74,216,154.

This was a done deal (so I, and most other sane people thought at the time), but interesting to watch as the election became official. Trump was to speak at a rally at noon, Washington D.C. time. What will he say, I wondered. That was one o'clock, Texas time. I took a lunch break.

After Jim and I had our usual sandwiches and chips with small talk, I said I was going to watch the proceedings in Washington. He said call me if anything exciting happens. He went back to work in his study, and I settled in my favorite chair in front of the TV, with my needlepoint. It was almost 2 p.m. Houston time.

There was the House of Representatives, in live coverage, real time. Nancy Pelosi, et al. Quiet hummings and buzzings, a Congress in session, ready to do its work. All was as it should be.

I threaded a new needle and started another section of my needlepoint pillow cover. It was a 2020 Christmas present from my husband, who had also given me one for Christmas 2017, when Donald Trump was President and half the nation was still in shock. I hadn't done needlepoint for twenty years or so, but I wanted something soothing and cheerful that year. That one was a cover for a sofa pillow, a picture of a baby lamb on a green field with a white fence. Very calming. This 2020 needlepoint I needed because of Covid and another nerve-wracking presidential election. It was another cushion cover, a picture of a boy sitting in a tree, playing a flute, with various birds and a squirrel in the tree, and two fat sheep grazing below. Very fanciful, very peaceful.

I stitched away, quite contented, glancing up now and then at the TV screen. A few minutes after 2 p.m. it suddenly it went dark, and a commentator's tense, uncertain voice said something like, "We have temporarily lost coverage. There are reports of protesters in the House chamber." Jim might want to see this, I said to myself, so I called to him to come and see. "Something's happening," I said. Was that ever an understatement!

What my husband and I saw when the picture came back on, was what everybody has seen replayed many times over since that day: chaos, mobs of people, mostly men, some weirdly costumed, some waving flags (some of those were Confederate battle flags), some with canes, clubs, and other weapons, swarming up the Capitol steps, climbing over barriers, smashing windows, breaking doors, bursting into the Capitol of the United States of America. That had not happened since British troops attacked the Capitol in the War of 1812.

Jim watched with me for a few minutes, and then retreated to his study. "Call me if something else happens," he said. What else could happen that would be worse than this, I thought. I pushed my needle into another square and kept watching the unbelievable unfold. A mob was storming the United States Capitol. Was I on the wrong channel? Was this some banana republic? I heard shouts of "Break it down! Break it down!" I saw beatings, I saw people running, panic-stricken, down marble stairs, down panelled hallways. I drew my needle through, pulling the yarn tight, feeling a little like Madame deFarge in Dickens' *A Tale of Two Cities*, the woman who knits as she watches the guillotine lop off heads in the French Revolution. Except that she was gleeful, and I was horrified.

As stunned newscasters tried desperately to stay calm and make sense of what was going on, I realized at first that they knew no more than I. The afternoon wore on. More violence. Shouts and loud unidentifiable noises. Reports of gas masks. A gun shot. Capitol police valiantly trying to control the mobs. Talk of National Guard troops, but they did not appear, because (as we learned later) Trump did not order them until the mayhem had been going on for more than two hours. I kept watching. At four o'clock I made myself a cup of tea. I kept watching. I could not bear to watch, and I could not stop watching. President-elect Biden spoke to the nation on national TV and asked President Trump (who was watching his own TV in the White House) to go on TV and ask the Capitol mob to stop. Instead, President Trump tweeted a video to the mob, saying he loved them, calling them "very special"— and telling them to go home.

Five hours after the break-in of the Capitol began, police and National Guard troops secured the building and restored a semblance of order.

Twitter and Facebook removed President Trump from their platforms.

At 11:32 p.m. Congress resumed its joint session.

At 3:42 a.m. January 7, 2021, Joseph R. Biden was certified as the winner of the 2020 presidential election.
Mission accomplished.

My fears about "the next two weeks" turned out to be groundless. We did get through those dark days, and on January 20, 2021, Joseph R. Biden was sworn in as the 46th President of the United States of America. His Vice-President was Kamala Harris, the first woman to hold that office. She was also the first woman of color to hold that office, but that's a story for another time.

In April 2022 there was another momentous "first." Kentanji Brown Jackson was confirmed as associate justice of the U.S .Supreme Court. She is the first woman of color to hold that office.

As I write this, we are a world on hold, as Russia ravages Ukraine in a war that may end badly—but for whom?

ABOUT THE AUTHOR

Virginia Bernhard is Professor Emerita of History at the University of St. Thomas, Houston. She is a co-author of two U.S. history textbooks, and the author of seven other books about American history. Her most recent book is *The Smell of War: Three Americans in the Trenches of World War I* (2018). Her historical novel about early Virginia, *A Durable Fire* (1990, 1991), was reissued as *Jamestown: the Novel* in 2014.

Dr. Bernhard is married to Houston actor/writer Jim Bernhard. They have three grown children.

Printed in Great Britain
by Amazon

82019169R00068